FAIRLAWN

Restoring the Splendor

TOM DAVIS

Library of Congress Catalog Card Number: 2001088285
ISBN: 0-915024-89-6
06 05 04 03 02 01   6 5 4 3 2 1

Editor: Judith A. Ettenhofer
Creative Director: Kathie Campbell
Production: Heather Larson and Carol Lynn Benoit

Photographic Credits
Jeff Frey & Associates: Dust Jacket (front), Chapter 1 (page left), p. 116
Douglas County Historical Society: Table of Contents (page left), pp. 2-49
City of Superior/Jeff Frey & Associates: Dust Jacket (back), Title Page, Table of Contents (page right), p. 84, pp. 90-115
City of Superior/Charles Cieslak, p. 59
LHB Engineers & Architects: p. 53, pp. 62-81, p. 87
Lake Superior Magazine: Illustrations, p. 25
Building Conservation Systems/Ronald Koenig: p. 82, p.88

Proceeds from the sale of this book benefit the Douglas County Historical Society.

Printed in China.

Trails Custom Publishing, a division of Trails Media Group, Inc.
P.O. Box 317 • Black Earth, WI 53515
(800) 236-8088 • e-mail: info@wistrails.com
www.wistrails.com

Dedication

DAVID EVANS   1948-1998

I never drive by or see a photograph of Fairlawn Mansion without thinking
about him. His leadership, vision and expertise are fingerprinted on this building.
This book is dedicated to the memory of David Evans, FAIA. David's sudden death
in August of 1998, during the restoration of Fairlawn, prevented him from seeing
his work in finished form.

David's passion was the preservation of this nation's historic resources.
He was also an excellent leader and visionary, who could easily inspire those around him.
I hope that as you read this book you will not only be inspired about the
preservation of our heritage, but that you will also remember, as David Evans did,
how one life—yours—can effect change in the lives of others.

James Scott Brew, AIA

FAIRLAWN

Table of Contents

Chapter One

The History of
SUPERIOR, WISCONSIN, AND OF MARTIN PATTISON

FROM THE FRONT STEPS of Fairlawn Mansion, Martin Pattison watched the 19th century end and the 20th century begin. He saw the Great Lakes schooners with their billowing acres of canvas give way to low-slung steel-hulled freighters; he heard the clip-clop of horses pulling hansom cabs replaced by the throaty belch of the automobile; he marveled as man took flight. It's easy to imagine him there, framed by the porch columns, gazing out across Lake Superior with those hawk-like eyes, the breeze cool even in summertime, the water exotically blue.

Given the change he witnessed, and how far he came to arrive at this place, he must have thought often of his days as a lumberman, directing crews as they felled the last of the virgin white pine along the Black River; or to his time rambling the wilderness of northern Minnesota with a 100-pound pack on his back, prospecting for iron and staking claim to the deposits that would make him rich, that would make him the man he became, that would give him the wherewithal to build Fairlawn.

Perhaps a slight smile came to his lips as he thought of those days; perhaps he gave an almost imperceptible shake of his head, recalling his life, considering the distance in time, and in station, that he'd traveled. And just as the story of Fairlawn cannot be told without telling the story of Martin Pattison, the story of Martin Pattison cannot be told without telling the story of Superior.

In the early 1890s, Superior, Wisconsin, was a city on the cusp of greatness. Its citizens could point with justifiable pride to the physical symbols of its ascendancy. Superior's monolithic grain elevators and mammoth docks for the loading of coal and iron were the world's largest. In an atmosphere charged by seemingly limitless economic growth, industrial expansion, and prosperity in general—it was the high-water mark of America's Gilded Age—they must have struck local residents as the modern equivalents of the fabled ancient wonders. These facilities (and scores of lesser ones) were served by a teeming nexus of railroads, which in turn were served by a more-or-less constant flow of ship traffic in and out of Superior's deep, well-protected harbor. Indeed, Superior soon took to calling itself "the place where rail meets sail," although the era of sail-powered vessels, with all its attendant glamour, was, of course, rapidly drawing to a close.

Be that as it may, what had been little more than a sleepy outpost on the northern frontier had transformed itself, virtually overnight, into a bona fide boomtown. Galvanized by the arrival of the railroads in the 1880s, its population exploded, multiplying from barely 9,000 in 1889 to 35,000 in 1892 and making Superior, for a time, the state's second-largest city, surpassed only by Milwaukee. The value of freight moved through its harbor more than doubled during this same period, from $28 million to $58 million, while the quantity of rail freight more than tripled, from 1.25 billion pounds to 4.21 billion pounds. The number of manufacturing establishments jumped from nine to 79. The largest of these, a shipyard called the American Steel Barge Works that specialized in the distinctive "whaleback" freighter, employed more than 1,200 people. The city boasted four daily newspapers, two cigar makers, four bottling companies, and at least two breweries.

The *Christopher Columbus,* the only "whaleback"-style steamboat built to ferry passengers, was launched by its designer, Capt. Alexander McDougall, on December 3, 1892, in West Superior.

Superior's dizzying growth did not go unnoticed elsewhere. Some of the wealthiest men in America—captains of industry, rail and lumber barons, men who strode the earth like giants—were persuaded to make significant investments in the area. James J. Hill of Great Northern Railroad fame (whose bronze likeness glowers at passersby on Belknap Street) and Standard Oil's John D. Rockefeller are perhaps the two most resonant names today, but there were many others who included this comparatively remote community carved out of the Lake Superior wilderness in their dreams of empire.

"A showing that cannot be surpassed by any other city in the world" was how the *Report of the City Statistician for 1892* characterized Superior's metamorphosis. Caught up in the fevered spirit of the day, local boosters began touting Superior as the "Chicago of the Northwest." (In those days, "the Northwest" customarily referred to the Great Lakes states—Ohio, Indiana, Illinois, Michigan, and Wisconsin—that composed the old Northwest Territory and marked the farthest extent of the United States in that direction prior to the Louisiana Purchase.)

It was a bold claim, one that from the vantage point of a century's worth of hindsight carries the faint whiff of the outrageous.

It was a bold claim, one that from the vantage point of a century's worth of hindsight carries the faint whiff of the outrageous. Given the evidence at the time, though, when America as a whole embraced the notion of progress as if it were the grail and equated civilization with industrialization, it was not entirely unreasonable. The frontier had been closed—or so said Wisconsin-born historian Frederick Jackson Turner, then at Harvard, in his famous pronouncement—and with the business of westward expansion ended there was no reason that Superior should not aspire to become one of the great cities of America. Or, for that matter, one of the great cities of the world.

This scenario was, if anything, even grander than the one envisioned by the city's founders, a consortium of land speculators that included financiers from Washington, Pittsburgh, and Philadelphia as well as Stephen A. Douglas, the Illinois senator best remembered for his debates with country lawyer Abraham Lincoln. (Douglas County, which includes Superior, was named for him in 1855). When plans were announced in 1852 to build a ship canal around the rapids at Sault Ste. Marie—rapids that had hindered, if not altogether prevented, water-borne commerce between Lake Superior and the rest of the Great Lakes (which were connected to New York City and the Atlantic Seaboard via the Erie Canal)—these men recognized the commercial potential of the harbor at the lake's extreme western end and moved quickly in response. The town site of Superior was officially platted and recorded in September 1854. The Soo Locks were dedicated in June of the following year, and by 1857 Superior's population had reached the 2,000 mark.

Superior had great aspirations in the 1890s to be the "Chicago of the Northwest."

But if the "modern" history of Superior began in the 1850s, the human history of the area called the "Head of the Lakes" began long before. For centuries, the wedge of land between the St. Louis and Nemadji rivers had been favored by indigenous peoples for its productive hunting, fishing, and ricing, its gentle topography, and its convenient access to the body of water known to the Ojibwe, the area's most recent occupants, as *Otchipwekitchigami*, "great sea of the Ojibwe." (Longfellow's "Gitchee-Gumee" was a reasonably close transcription, although Hiawatha, the name he chose for the hero of his eponymous epic poem, was not Ojibwe but Iroquois.)

The first Europeans to arrive were the French. Their explorations during the 17th century were fueled by the lucrative fur trade and the lingering possibility of discovering the fabled Northwest Passage to the Pacific Ocean and, eventually, the Orient. In 1615, Samuel de Champlain, upon "discovering" Lake Huron, was astonished to find that its waters were not salt, as he expected, but fresh. The endless blue horizon initially convinced him that he had indeed made his way to the Pacific Ocean. Putting the water to his lips convinced him that he had in fact discovered something entirely new, something entirely beyond the realm of European experience. He called this inland ocean *La Mer Douce*, "The Sweet Sea."

A few years later, Etienne Brulé, whom Champlain had dispatched to do further reconnaissance in this vast and brooding wilderness, returned to Montreal bearing tales of another Sweet Sea to the north. As the general configuration of the Great Lakes gradually revealed itself, this "Sweet Sea of the North," *Mer Douce du Nord*, was re-christened *Lac Superieur*. Not because it was the largest—it would take a while before that could be proved—but because it was uppermost in the interconnected system.

There is sketchy evidence that Brulé may have visited the western end of Lake Superior during this officially sanctioned expedition of the early 1620s, and even sketchier evidence that he may have laid eyes on the site of present-day Superior during a previous unsanctioned foray in the mid-1610s. But there is no doubt whatsoever that his successors in the line of French exploration, Pierre-Esprit Radisson and Médard Chouart, Sieur Des Groseilliers, had begun trading with the local Indians by the mid-1650s, fully 200 years before Senator Douglas and his partners staked their claims. Jesuit missionaries, called "Black Robes" by the Ojibwe, followed close on their heels. The most notable of them was Father Claude Allouez, who arrived in the area in 1655 and whose name survives in a number of Superior-area landmarks.

The toehold gained by Radisson and Groseilliers—"We were Caesars," crowed the

Trolleys transported Superior's 35,000 residents around the city in the 1890s.

Prior to its industrial growth boom, Superior was marked by a stockade, built during 1882-83 by the state of Wisconsin, to guard against Sioux Indian attacks. Photograph by David F. Barry, from a drawing.

Opposite: The arrival of the first street cars in South Superior, on September 14, 1892, sparked a celebration and street barbecue.

former in one of his journals—was strengthened and consolidated by Daniel Greysolon. Better remembered by his honorary title, Sieur du Lhut, he gave his name to the modern city of Duluth, Minnesota. (Together, Superior and Duluth are known today as the Twin Ports.) Greysolon led an expedition to the western end of Lake Superior in 1679, his mission being to bring the Sioux—or, more accurately, the lands to the west that they controlled and the fur they were in a position to provide—into the French fold. By brokering a peace agreement between them and their longtime enemies, the Ojibwe, he succeeded.

Superior remained a small but important fur-trading outpost as it passed from French to British rule in the wake of the French and Indian War of 1763, and from British to American control following the Revolutionary War and the Northwest Ordinance of 1787. It was handy to two of the fur trade's main thoroughfares: the Grand Portage, which connected the Great Lakes to Hudson's Bay, and the St. Croix Trail, which led to the Mississippi River and the Gulf of Mexico. The Hudson's Bay Company, the Northwest Company, and John Jacob Astor's American Fur Company all maintained posts in Superior at one time or another.

At the time the town was platted in 1854, however, the trading posts had moved elsewhere, and Superior was essentially uninhabited. Rapid early growth stalled out and actually regressed in the face of the nationwide financial upheaval known as the Panic of 1857, the Civil War, and the unrest created by the Sioux uprising in neighboring Minnesota in

1862. It was not until the 1880s that Superior began to rebound—but it did so with a vengeance. The catalyst was the arrival, in 1881, of the first railroad to serve the community, the Northern Pacific. More railroads rushed to follow, notably Hill's Great Northern and its subsidiary lines, and as docks, elevators, warehouses, and other appurtenances of commerce bloomed in their wake, Superior became a vital link in the transportation of western raw materials to eastern mills and markets.

In 1889, Superior was formally incorporated as a city. The first man to serve as mayor was one Alexander McRae. The second, elected in 1890, was the man who built Fairlawn, Martin Pattison.

It was fitting that Martin Pattison should be elected mayor, as he was by all accounts Superior's leading citizen. He was a man of his times and a man for his times, a man who embodied the baronial virtues that prominent public figures of the Gilded Age were expected to display. He was affluent, yes—fabulously so—but he was philanthropic in equal measure. At ease in the most exclusive company, he also seems to have retained the common touch. If he did not wear his prosperity lightly—completed in 1891 at a reported cost of $150,000, Fairlawn was far and away the city's grandest residence—at least he wore it well.

Pattison's enthusiasms were many, and he embraced them robustly: At age 60, he and several companions took a month-long, 600-mile canoe trip through the wilds of northern Ontario. He enjoyed hunting, fishing, boating, and curling; he collected unusual minerals and Indian artifacts; he maintained a rustic getaway, known as "The Leisure Lodge," on Burntside Lake near Ely, Minnesota; he supported numerous charitable causes (including churches) and was a member of several fraternal organizations. He also found time to devote to his wife, Grace, and their six children. Two other children—each a twin daughter to surviving daughters—died in infancy.

A staunch Republican somewhat in the Teddy Roosevelt mold, Pattison had served a term as sheriff of Douglas County before he was elected mayor of Superior. Earlier, he'd been a school board member in Sanilac County, Michigan, and a state legislator there. He would eventually serve three one-year terms as mayor—re-elected in 1891, he dropped out of the race in '92, lost by a narrow margin in '93, and after "retiring" from politics came back to serve his third and final term in '96—and helping to engineer Superior's transformation from a frontier boomtown into a mature, respectable, thoroughly "modern" city seemed to satisfy his political ambitions. Pattison was recruited to run for lieutenant governor on at least two occasions, but both times he declined.

Photographs of Martin Pattison in his later years show a man with a patrician air, his angular features accentuated by a long, aquiline nose, arched eyebrows, and full beard trimmed to a neat point. It is a malleable face, capable of conveying both a kindly, avuncular receptivity and a cool, piercing intelligence. The wisdom is almost palpable, but it is the kind of Old Testament wisdom that sheaths a whetted wrath. His eyes are deep set, inscrutable. Even when he is balancing a granddaughter on his knee, he gives the impression of a man not to be trifled with.

Martin Pattison was born on January 17, 1841, in southern Ontario. Some sources give his place of birth as Niagara County, site of the famous falls. Others say Haldimand County, farther west on the north shore of Lake Erie. There is no disagreement whatsoever, though, over the fact that Martin Pattison was not his birth name. The name to which he answered until he was in his early 30s, in fact—was Simeon Martin Thayer. Pattison was the maiden name of his mother, Emmarilla, whose family tree reportedly shared a common root with Benjamin Franklin's.

His father, also named Simeon, came from a long line of American-born Thayers, including yet another Simeon who was a general in the Revolutionary War. The family of young Simeon Martin did not stay in Canada long. When he was just entering his teens, circa 1853, they moved across the border to a farm in Sanilac County on Michigan's

Martin Pattison.

"thumb." Farming seemed to hold little appeal for him, however, and at the age of 17, presumably having gone as far as he could go in the local public schools, he took a job in a logging camp. This line of work suited him—it was the beginning of the lumber boom that swept across the northern Great Lakes region in the latter half of the 19th century—and by 1866 he and a partner, an Irish immigrant named Joseph Murdock, had set up their own lumber operation near Minden City, Michigan.

It was at about this time that Simeon Martin Thayer's political ambitions began to manifest themselves. He served for six years on the Minden City School Board, which seems a little curious given the fact that for the first four of those years he was a bachelor and had no children of his own. His status changed on August 7, 1869, when he married Joe Murdock's sister, Isabella. The first of their two children, a daughter named Zelia, was born December 18, 1869.

This line of work suited him—it was the beginning of the lumber boom that swept across the northern Great Lakes region in the latter half of the 19th century.

Opposite: Thriving Superior's industries in 1896 included the Webster Chair Manufacturing Co.

The rigid Victorian morality so often associated with the 19th century was apparently not in force there, and/or then. Which is to say, there seem to have been no repercussions—none in the public realm, anyway—over the timing of the wedding, or of Zelia's birth. Simeon Martin Thayer continued to serve on the Minden City School Board, and in 1871 the local body politic elected him as its representative to the Michigan Legisla-

ture. At the age of 30, he was a bona fide up-and-comer, a young man with a bright future, a figure who bore watching.

Then, for reasons that will likely never be known but which offer tantalizing opportunities for speculation, Simeon Martin Thayer left his wife and children (son Joseph was born May 5, 1872), beat a hasty retreat from Sanilac County, and began going by the name Martin Pattison. According to accounts published during his lifetime (accounts that make no mention of his name change or previous family), he moved in 1872 to the vicinity of Marquette, in Michigan's Upper Peninsula, where he re-established himself as a lumberman and also began a fledgling mining business. His partner in this enterprise was his younger brother, William, who had been involved in the construction of railroads in Iowa. He, too, changed his surname from Thayer to Pattison.

There is, however, an alternative account of Martin Pattison's abrupt exit from Lower Michigan, and his subsequent whereabouts. This deliciously scandalous allegation, which Isabella Thayer made public in 1890—shortly after Pattison's first mayoral triumph in Superior—asserts that her husband ran off with her sister, first to Salt Lake City, then to San Francisco, and that he remained in the West for several years until he surfaced in Marquette under his new name.

Regardless of what—or whom—one chooses to believe, the fact of the matter is that Martin Pattison didn't get around to divorcing Isabella Thayer until June of 1890, at which point he'd been married to the former Grace Emma Frink, the daughter of a Great Lakes lighthouse keeper, for nearly 11 years. (Actually, it was Mrs. Thayer who petitioned for and received the divorce, on grounds of "desertion.") Pattison was 38, Grace Frink 23 when they married in November 1879, in her hometown of Marquette. The inescapable conclusion is that Martin Pattison was determined to build a new life for himself, and in order to do that he had to wipe the slate clean—at least insofar as the rest of the world was concerned.

Martin Pattison's first wife, Isabella Murdock, and their children, Joseph and Zelia. Pattison apparently abandoned this family about 1872.

Even when the rest of the world became aware that Martin Pattison had a skeleton or two clattering in his closet, it was quite willing to consign this knowledge to the past and focus instead on the progressive steps he was taking in the present, steps that were helping to usher Superior into the 20th century. While tongues undoubtedly wagged when Isabella Thayer emerged from the shadows in 1890—one can only imagine the effect on Grace, and on the Pattisons' relationship—her revelations weren't sufficiently bothersome to the citizens of Superior to dissuade them from re-electing Pattison mayor a year later. Maybe it was as simple as this: They knew a good thing when they saw it.

Still, he does seem to have led something of a charmed life. In November 1898, he and three companions were fishing on Burntside Lake, where Pattison had purchased a pine-studded island in 1892 and built his rustic Leisure Lodge a year later. Someone hooked a fish, and in the ensuing commotion their canoe capsized. This begs the question of why an experienced outdoorsman like Martin Pattison would assent to cramming four anglers into a single canoe, especially in November, when the water was on the verge of freezing. Whatever the answer, two of the men, Jack West and F.C. Hamen, drowned before a party of Ojibwe camped on a nearby island—a party led by Pattison's longtime friend, "Chief" Joe Boshey—heard their cries for help and paddled out to rescue them. (The Leisure Lodge, by the way, still stands, and it's still owned by members of the Pattison family.)

Considering the evidence, it's tempting to argue that Martin Pattison was somehow fated to settle in Superior, strike it rich, become mayor, build Fairlawn, and do all the other things he did to leave his mark on history—a mark that, by any reckoning, remains an overwhelmingly positive one. The idea of "destiny," of course, meaning a kind of pre-ordained unfolding of events toward a specific end, was much in vogue during the 19th century, and in this respect he was indeed a man of and for his times. Seizing what amounted to a second chance when he married Grace and moved to northwestern Wisconsin, Pattison made the best of it. He is open to criticism, certainly. But during his

Isabella Murdock Thayer

entire nearly 40-year tenure in Superior, Martin Pattison seems to have been deeply and genuinely committed to promoting the public good.

Early in his first term as mayor, for example, he curtailed a potentially "vicious" labor strike by allying himself with local working men, many of whom were Scandinavian immigrants, and spearheading a resolution raising the minimum wage from $1.75 to $2 per day for all construction contracted by the city. At the conclusion of his second term in office in 1892, an editorial in *The Inland Ocean*, one of several newspapers then published in Superior, lauded his record: "When Mr. Pattison first became mayor, the city had one mile of street paving and about the same amount of sewerage, but at the close of his second administration there were 13 miles of paved streets and over 40 miles of sewerage. During his regime the city made the most rapid strides toward industrial and commercial supremacy that it has in its history."

Another paper summed up his third and final mayoral stint in 1896-97 as follows: "Mr. Pattison ... goes out of office leaving the city in the best financial shape, not a dollar of floating debt, sinking funds all full, not an unsold bond, no unfinished contracts, the fire department fully equipped, the credit of the city OK and three-quarters of a million dollars in the Treasury."

Martin and Grace left Marquette for Superior within a few months of their marriage. They were joined there by Martin's brother, William, and in the early 1880s the Pattisons ran a white pine logging operation on the Black River, about 12 miles south of the city. Many years later, after having been sold and then re-acquired, some of this same land would be part of a 660-acre gift that Martin Pattison gave to the people of Wisconsin, a gift that included the fourth-highest waterfall east of the Rockies, 165-foot Big Manitou, and that would eventually form the core of Pattison State Park.

The Pattison brothers divested themselves of their logging interests in 1882 in order to focus on prospecting for iron in the wilds of northern Minnesota. It's said that they

Grace Pattison

With his financial needs well in hand, Martin Pattison once again decided to throw his hat into the political ring.

Superior, still thriving at the end of World War I, erected a "victory arch" of lights.

would shoulder 100-pound packs and set out on foot up the 90-mile trail that led from Duluth north to the village of Tower, at the foot of the Vermilion Range. Crisscrossing that vast, rock-hewn mosaic of glittering blue lakes and trackless spruce forests, they discovered and laid claim to the veins of ore that would be developed as the Chandler and Pioneer mines—ore that would help feed the rapidly industrializing nation's ravenous appetite for steel and would make the Pattison brothers rich beyond their wildest dreams.

With his financial needs well in hand, Martin Pattison once again decided to throw his hat into the political ring. He ran successfully for sheriff of Douglas County in 1884, and although he served only a single term, he distinguished himself, according to *The Inland Ocean*, as "an honest and capable official." He also put himself squarely in the public eye, thus laying the groundwork for later political campaigns.

By 1888, although he'd been in the Superior area for less than ten years, Pattison had established himself as one of its best-known and most highly regarded citizens. An article in *The Superior Times*, dated March 24 of that year, essentially a testimonial to his achievements and character, reads in part: "(A)lthough Mr. Pattison is credited with a great deal of honor for his pioneer work on the Vermilion (Range), he still deserves far more than

he will ever receive ...

"At present he is living at Superior, where he has a comfortable home and an estimable family. Socially, he is an affable, pleasing gentleman, gives credit to the party deserving it, and does not seek to detract from the reputation of any man ...

"He is a man of liberal, broad views, and a person that creates friends while reaping a fortune. Cases of this kind are few as the opposite generally rules."

It was around this time that Martin and Grace decided to quit their "comfortable" home on West 3rd and build the palatial Victorian mansion they would christen Fairlawn. The Pattisons had by then toured Europe, where they were exposed to the art, architecture, and culture that, by dint of its self-assured elegance and multi-layered sophistication, set the standard for the entire world. It seems likely, too, that they were aware of the grand residences in places like Chicago, Milwaukee, and Minneapolis-St. Paul. Money attracts (and begets) money, and as the news of his iron strikes spread, doors both figurative and literal likely opened for them. In a fine 1999 article on Martin Pattison and Fairlawn for *Lake Superior* magazine, Hugh Bishop wrote, "There is no doubt that the Pattisons purposely set out to make this a model home for others of the nouveau riche class in the burgeoning Midwest, sparing no expense ..."

The Pattisons purchased an entire city block fronted by what was then called Bay Street. Befitting their stature in the community, the site afforded a commanding view of Superior Bay and, beyond the sandspit of Minnesota Point, the headlands of the North Shore and the big lake itself, sprawling into a blue infinity. A note in *The Superior Times*, dated August 31, 1889, reads, "Martin Pattison expects to award the contract for his new residence today, and get the work begun next week ... It will be a very beautiful building of brown stone and all the modern fixtures for conveniences ... We do not know of anyone more worthy to enjoy such a home than Mr. and Mrs. Pattison, and we trust they may live long to enjoy it." ◆

Opposite: Superior—"the last possible great marine city in the interior of North America."

FAIRLAWN

Chapter Two

The Building
OF FAIRLAWN MANSION

IN THE EARLY 1890s, its population having nearly quadrupled in a period of less than five years, Superior was poised to stake its claim as the industrial, commercial, and transportation hub of the western Great Lakes. And with the transition from a raw, rugged outpost on the wild northern frontier to a bustling modern city in the mainstream of American culture all but complete, the construction of Martin Pattison's baronial mansion was a kind of capstone, the final, tangible proof of Superior's stature. It may have been the property of the Pattisons, but it seems to have been a point of pride among the citizenry at large, a symbol not just of private wealth, but of public achievement.

It is not surprising, then, that the local newspapers kept close tabs on the mansion's progress. On October 26, 1889, *The Superior Times* reported, "The foundation of Mr. Pattison's new residence is above the ground and will soon be ready for the next step to be taken." An update in the November 16 paper read, "Martin Pattison let the contract for the carpenter work on his new residence last Tuesday to Fred A. Dole for about $12,000. Mr. Dole is a number one workman and is taking the best jobs now going. He will soon complete his work on the Conan mansion, and his work there will compare favorably with anything at the head of the lake."

The Conan mansion belonged to Dr. William Conan, a Superior dentist whom the Pattison brothers had recruited as a partner in the development of the Chandler and Pioneer mines in Minnesota. In fact, Fred Dole was the builder of choice for all three of the partners, having also supervised the construction of a fine home for William Pattison. Each of the partners' estates was on Bay Street, overlooking the water; sadly, the Conan and William Pattison mansions were razed in the early 1960s.

One of the enduring mysteries surrounding Fairlawn is the identity of its architect. None of the construction blueprints survives—or at least none has ever surfaced—nor is anyone specifically credited in the newspaper accounts of the day. Informed speculation, however, centers around one John DeWaard, who was listed as an architect in the city directories for both Superior and Duluth and is known to have designed

"An Elegant Home—Mayor Pattison's New House and its Appointments"

some of the decorative woodwork that adorns Fairlawn's interior. In addition, several buildings positively attributed to DeWaard exhibit stylistic similarities to Fairlawn.

Construction continued through 1890—the year Martin Pattison was first elected mayor—and into 1891. On May 16 of that year, the *Superior Evening Telegram* published a long, breathlessly effulgent article headlined "An Elegant Home—Mayor Pattison's New House and its Appointments." Although another three-and-a-half months would elapse before Fairlawn was ready for occupancy, and while many of the draperies, floor coverings, furnishings, and *objets d'art* remained to be installed, the mansion's effect on the anonymous author of the piece was clearly overwhelming. Dazzled though this scribe may have been, however, the account he penned of Fairlawn as it originally appeared is both historically important and wondrously evocative. Abridged for length and slightly edited, it reads as follows:

"If Mayor Pattison had sought through all the northwest he could not have found a more beautiful spot for a residence than the one now graced by the mansion he has erected on the shores of Superior Bay. The view from the house and grounds includes everything in nature, from the ruggedly grand to the picturesque beauty of the softest meadow landscape. Old Lake Superior presents its ever varying face shining or storm-tossed over the fringe of Minnesota Point, and that same dark fringe and shining sands below make a fitting background for the placid surface of Superior Bay. Over to the north, the rocky shore rises to a mountainous height, and fills out an outline that would else be lacking in this charming picture. The prospect is delightful.

"The house itself is almost finished. Its architectural style belongs to the Renaissance, as indeed do the interior decorations. The facade is pleasing, particularly so where artistic ornamentation has added to the architectural design—but when once the massive mahogany portals are passed, and from the mosaic tiling of the vestibule one gets a glimpse into the splendid hall, in its baronial proportions and rich oak finish, the exterior is forgotten. To the right and left are doors leading into sitting room, library, parlor and music room, and at the farther end in an elevated alcove is a fireplace while the massive stairway turns up to the right. It doesn't require a very excited imagination to fill this grand apartment—for it is more apartment than hall—with the rich hangings and elegant appointments with which it is to be fitted, and with a blazing fire in the grate the completed picture would be the most charming, coziest place in the world to come into when old Superior is on the rampage and winter is on the outside. The most desirable thing in a fine house is a hall that befits it, and the hall in Mayor Pattison's house is simply magnificent.

"The sitting room to the right is a fine room with an open fireplace and finished in natural cherry. Just behind it is the library, a beautiful room finished in mahogany, a considerable portion of one side being filled by a fireplace set in a handsome piece of Egyptian marble and mountain silver. On the opposite side of the hall is the parlor—and the

Opposite: The magnificence of Fairlawn is evident in this photograph taken from the northeast after the conservatory was added during 1894-95.

Page 18: It wasn't until the 1990s, 100 years after Fairlawn was built, that ambitious plans began to coalesce to restore the mansion to its original splendor.

elegance of the taste displayed in the designing of the interior is shown to the greatest advantage in this room. The woodwork is birch and is elaborately and beautifully carved in artistic designs drawn by Mr. DeWaard. The delicate and beautiful nature of the tracery is easily shown in the length of time consumed by the carvers in the finishing. A small fortune is represented in the fireplace alone, which is mounted in gold and consists of the finest slab of Mexican onyx in the state. Through an archway that in its wealth of carving challenges delight, one passes into the music room, a large, light, airy apartment. The arch separating the rooms will, instead of doors, be fitted with a screen painted to represent the seasons—a valuable work of art. From this room a conservatory will extend along the side of the house, have access into the parlor and a perfect promenade acquired. A whole forest has been searched to find suitable woods for the exquisite paneled doors leading from the music room to the hall, and the result is a marvel in bird's-eye maple.

"A dining room to the rear of the music room is of a size that bespeaks the most hospitable intentions of the owner of the mansion. It is finished as it should be, in good substantial oak, with a sideboard built into the wall, so massive in its proportions as to shadow forth future feasts of most bounteous cheer.

"On the second floor are the chambers for the family and visitors' rooms. One room is finished in white and gold and the ceiling has been painted in delicate floral designs by an artist with a well-deserved reputation and who has done wonderfully clever work lying on his back on a scaffolding; a second room is in curly maple with natural finish, the ceiling ornate with festoons of roses and trailing vines. The easternmost suite, a bedroom, dressing room and alcove, forms the private apartment of the master of the house. The rooms are handsomely finished, the walls in heliotrope; white daisies and roses entwine the tinted ceiling. Above stairs again are more sleeping rooms, a dance hall and billiard room, either of which is large enough for the ground plan of a good-sized house, and up under the roof is a play room for the children.

Opposite: Martin and Grace Pattison and their six surviving children, with their families, posed for this portrait on the stair landing at Fairlawn about 1910.

"The basement is by no means uninteresting. There is the laundry with its stationary tubs, the bowling alley, a plunge bath of noble proportions, the servants' baths, an immense furnace and a gas machine. The plumbing, ventilation and sanitation was planned by one of the best-known experts in the country and is perfect. A thousand little things go to make this modern house the most perfect, when ready for occupancy next September, of any house within some hundreds of miles of its location."

On September 5, 1891, *The Superior Times* reported, "Mayor Pattison got moved into his new mansion on Thursday of this week and will in a few days be 'at home' to his friends in the most elegant home at the head of the lake."

The figure most frequently given as the cost for constructing Fairlawn is $150,000—a staggering sum for a private residence in that day and age. If anything, though, it's too conservative. In a family genealogy prepared in the late 1920s, a biographical sketch of Grace Pattison states, with reference to the mansion, "The total cost of building, equipment, and decoration was over a quarter of a million dollars."

Fairlawn was an architectural marvel, a showcase for the decorative arts—and a triumph of engineering. Virtually every "modern" convenience available at the time was incorporated into its construction. It was wired for electricity and piped for natural gas. Indeed, many of the interior lights were "combination" fixtures that could be operated via either source of energy. An electric elevator ran between the second floor, where the bedrooms

Opposite: Only Fairlawn's first floor has been restored to its original opulence; hopes are to restore the second and third floors eventually.

and bathrooms were located, and the basement laundry room, enabling the domestic staff to discreetly change the linens. (Make no mistake: To maintain a place like Fairlawn, an extensive staff—maids, cooks, nannies, butlers, groundskeepers, etc.—was a necessity, not a luxury.) Other amenities included nine gas-fueled fireplaces, hot and cold running water, steam heat and, last but by no means least, full indoor plumbing.

There was also a large carriage house, set off at a respectful distance south and west of the mansion itself and presumably built at about the same time. The Pattisons' original horse-drawn carriages were eventually replaced by those of the horseless variety. Unfortunately, with the exception of a few photographs that show partial views of the exterior, scant documentation of this structure, which was destroyed by fire in 1960, remains.

Such is not the case, happily, for the only other "outbuilding" associated with Fairlawn. Under the headline "Fairlawn Conservatory—Martin Pattison Will Build a Beautiful One This Spring," an article in the February 3, 1894, *Evening Telegram* reported the following:

"John Chisholm, the architect, has just completed the plans and specifications for a handsome conservatory to be erected by Martin Pattison on the east side of Fairlawn. The main structure will be 25x50 (feet) with a potting house 14x16 connecting the conservatory with the residence. The building will have a stone foundation, while the superstructure will consist wholly of iron, sheet laths and glass. On the inside will be an oval, 11x35, with a concrete walk 3-1/2 feet wide surrounding. In the oval there will be the necessary arrangements for the exhibition of flowers. The building will have a dome roof made of iron and plate glass and will be 15 feet high.

"The contracts for the work have nearly all been awarded. James Dever of the East End will put in the foundation while eastern firms will put in the iron and glass. The conservatory when completed will cost $4,500.

"Mr. Pattison has made arrangements for several thousand dollars worth of rare exotics

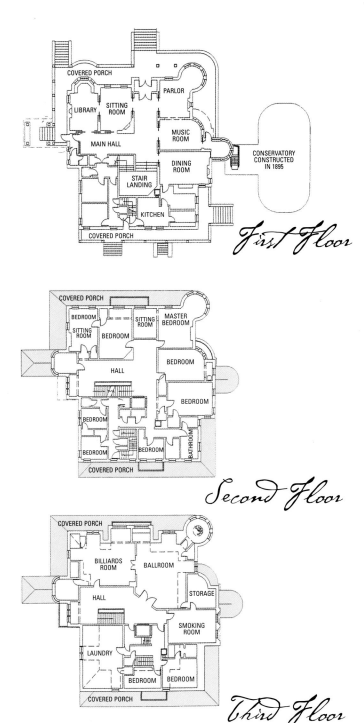

First Floor

Second Floor

Third Floor

and beautiful plants and flowers from the tropics which will adorn the conservatory. When completed the conservatory will be the finest in the Northwest."

In addition to the details it provides about the conservatory's design and construction, the article is significant in that it refers to the Pattison estate as "Fairlawn." While it seems doubtful that this was the first such reference to appear in print, it's perhaps the first documented one. It was customary, of course, for mansions of this scale to be given names by their owners, but precisely when the Pattisons began calling their place Fairlawn—and how they came up with this title—is another of those unanswered questions.

Opposite: Fairlawn, viewed from the southeast.

The completion of the conservatory brought Fairlawn to full flower. Architecturally, the 42-room mansion embodied virtually every important element associated with the Queen Anne style, which had its genesis in the 1870s as a distinctly American response to English Victorian designs and would remain in vogue until about 1910. Variety, multiplicity, and asymmetry are among the hallmarks of the Queen Anne home, along with what can only be described as a kind of glorious excess. As John Maass puts it in his *The Victorian Home in America*, "The American Queen Anne house is one of the most complex habitations ever devised for commoners."

He elaborates: "It rejected the traditional concept of unity in design, deliberately contrasting shapes, textures, and colors—solid and void, in and out, square and round, light and dark, rough and smooth. The ground plan is irregular, each facade has a different ele-

vation, and the roof, with its intersecting ridges and turrets, is a problem in solid geometry. The ground floor may be stone trimmed with brick, or brick trimmed with stone; the second story is faced with clapboards and shingles; the third story often features half-timbered gables, topped by a roof of vari-colored slate. There are porches, overhangs, bay windows, oriels, balconies, leaded glass, stained glass, plaster relief panels, dormers, turrets, towers, and clustered brick chimneys. Paradoxically, this busy allover pattern created a unity of its own, very much like a patchwork quilt that makes a strong design out of many different fabrics."

With a few minor exceptions—a wood-shingled roof and the absence of oriel windows, for example—Maass's "generic" description fits Fairlawn to the proverbial T. And because the assigning of architectural styles is by no means an exact science, there are those who label Fairlawn not simply a Queen Anne, but a Queen Anne with Chateauesque elements. The Chateauesque style, which took its inspiration from, as you might guess, the classic French chateau, was popular during roughly the same period (circa 1860s to 1910) and shared numerous similarities—turrets, dormers, balconies, etc.—with the Queen Anne style.

Literally from the ground up, Fairlawn's exterior incorporated noteworthy details. The foundation, for instance, was laid of brownstone—the vernacular name for the rust-colored sandstone found in the region—from the Acadia Quarry in nearby Amnicon. (Brownstone from this area of Wisconsin—often referred to as "Lake Superior brownstone"—was a fashionable building material in many parts of the country during the late 19th and early 20th centuries.) The porch featured grooved wooden columns with Corinthian capitals, as well as a coffered ceiling. Overlapping "fish scale" shakes covered much of the second and third floors and gave the mansion the "gingerbread" look commonly associated with the Victorian era. The second floor overhangs were supported by gracefully curved console brackets with the profile of stringed instruments, while the frieze that ran along the roof cornice was a band of copper, patinated to a rich green and

impressed with an ornate bull's-eye motif. Atop the cylindrical, multi-fenestrated tower soared an octagonal turret, a space that would please an Arthurian maiden. And at the peak of the uppermost gable on the front of the mansion, a copper tympanum bore the date 1890 in raised numerals.

For all its ornamentation, detail, and sheer architectural flourish, Fairlawn's exterior presented a vaguely stern, fortress-like aspect. It was almost as if Martin Pattison, while granting the necessity of its many purely aesthetic touches, wanted his home first and foremost to convey an impression of solidity and substance—and to convey this impression in no uncertain terms. Every home of this scale is, in a very real sense, a projection of the personality of its master, and in this respect Fairlawn can be viewed not only as a monument to Pattison's wealth and taste, but as the physical, tangible expression of his character.

Inside, however, past the "massive mahogany portals" of the outer doors and through the vestibule, where the initials "MP" appeared in flowing scroll on the mosaic tiled floor, Fairlawn showed a very different side—a side of unbridled, unrestrained, quintessentially Gilded Age opulence. There were curtains and draperies of fine damask edged with ball fringe; wall-to-wall carpets in a variety of elegant motifs; chandeliers and sconces of the most elaborate design; intricately carved, lustrously polished woodwork of oak, cherry, birch, mahogany, and bird's-eye maple; cornice friezes with delicately raised designs finished in gold leaf; exquisitely painted ceilings with plaster moldings; fireplaces faced with tile, marble, and onyx and trimmed with silver; sliding "pocket" doors that disappeared into the walls; sumptuously upholstered chairs, settees, and banquettes; potted palms and other exotic plants; tapestries, oil paintings in ornate gilt frames, marble statuary, stained and leaded glass; and on, and on, and on. The impact of this dazzlingly lavish scheme was staggering, and while it may appear over-the-top by today's post-Modern, post-Industrial standards, it was utterly de rigueur for the late Victorian period, when more was almost always better in the circles among which people like the Pattisons moved.

Opposite: A statue of Pandora, which today graces the parlor, is visible in this c. 1920 Ralph Greenfield photograph of the main hall, looking toward the west porte-cochere entrance.

These specifics of the mansion's original interior décor were documented in a series of outstanding photographs taken in the mid-1890s by David F. Barry. And therein lies a fascinating story. Prior to moving to Superior in 1890 and establishing a studio there (further evidence of Superior's reputation as a city on the move), Barry had operated out of Bismarck, in what was then known as the Dakota Territory. Born in upstate New York in 1854, Barry arrived in Bismarck just in time to photograph its most famous resident, George Armstrong Custer, before he marched west from Fort Abraham Lincoln and, along the banks of the Little Bighorn River in southwestern Montana, led five companies of the 7th Cavalry to destruction—and unintended immortality—on June 25, 1876.

The specifics of the mansion's original interior décor were documented in a series of outstanding photographs taken in the mid-1890s by David F. Barry.

Subsequently, as the Sioux were forced onto reservations, Barry sought out and photographed such renowned chiefs as Sitting Bull, Red Cloud, Gall, and many others. He earned their trust as well—"Little Shadow-Catcher," they called him—and by so doing was able to persuade them to share their memories of the Battle of the Little Bighorn. Written down, these memories would eventually become a rich source of information for such Custer biographers as Evan Connell, author of *Son of the Morning Star*.

Barry trained his lens on the likes of Buffalo Bill Cody, too, and in addition to portraits he captured numerous scenes depicting military, pioneer, and Indian life on the Great Plains. Today, the Barry oeuvre is recognized as one of the most important pictorial records of that time and place in existence, and only Edward S. Curtis (a Wisconsin native, coincidentally) is ranked ahead of him as a photographer of the American Indian. (The Douglas County Historical Society owns an extensive collection of Barry photographs, including his iconic images of Sitting Bull and Red Cloud.)

Barry's pictures would serve as invaluable guides to the team involved in the restoration process, assisting them in replicating the mansion's original appearance in the most authentic and accurate way possible.

Although Barry continued to portray Indians as the opportunity arose after relocating to Superior—he lived there until his death in 1934—he essentially settled into a comfortable career as a mainstream commercial photographer. It was certainly provident of the Pattisons to have him photograph the interior of Fairlawn. In addition to their importance as historical documents, Barry's pictures would serve as invaluable guides to the team involved in the restoration process, assisting them in replicating the mansion's original appearance in the most authentic and accurate way possible. Another series of photos, these taken by the Greenfield studio in the late 1910s, reveal the changes—minor, for the most part—made by the Pattisons over the course of their occupancy.

While the existence of these photographs can only be considered a blessing, it's a bit unfortunate that they begin—and end—with the first floor. To be sure, this is where the mansion's major "public" spaces were, the rooms that showcased the Pattisons' affluence and sophistication, so it's not surprising that they desired to have them photographed for posterity. And given the prudish mores of the day, admitting a camera into their bedrooms, no matter how innocent the intent, may well have been unthinkable. Be that as it may, there are no known photographs that depict the interiors of Fairlawn's second and third floors—or the basement, with its bowling alley and "plunge bath of noble proportions"—as they appeared during the nearly 30 years the Pattisons lived there.

The Pattisons raised six children at Fairlawn. Four were already in tow when they moved in—Martha, Byron (the only son), Ethel, and Alice—with Myrna and Lois entering the world in 1892 and '93, respectively. Both Myrna's twin, Vyrna, and Lois's twin, Leda, died in infancy.

These traumas aside, the Pattisons' life at Fairlawn undoubtedly appeared idyllic to the outside world, and, in particular, to the working-class families that made up the vast majority of Superior's population. In many respects it probably *was* idyllic. One imagines Easter egg hunts and garden parties, ladies' teas in the parlor, formal dinners followed by dancing in the third-floor ballroom, recitals in the music room, the mansion decked out foundation-to-turret in holiday finery, the magical smells of gingerbread and mulled cider wafting from the kitchen. At least four weddings took place at Fairlawn, including daughter Ethel's and the 1896 double wedding of nieces Mary Anna Gowling and Eva Irene Thayer. (Today, in the wake of its restoration, Fairlawn is again a popular venue for weddings.)

Another noteworthy event was the gala reception the Pattisons hosted for son Byron and his bride, the former Grace Bamfield, in the autumn of 1901. To the surprise of both families, the couple announced that they'd been married in secret that June, after which Byron returned to his studies at the Michigan School of Mines in Houghton (now Michi-

Previous pages 34-35: Gilded Age opulence marked Fairlawn's every room, from the bird's-eye maple doorway and detailed ceiling painting of the music room (left), to the Mexican onyx fireplace and carved birch woodwork of the parlor (right).

gan Technological University), and Grace resumed living with her parents in Denver. (The Bamfields had moved there from Superior, where Grace and Byron were high school sweethearts.) When Byron finally came clean to his father, the *Evening Telegram* reported, "Martin Pattison is quite a philosopher and he of course made no objection." Given the fact that his own marriage scandal had been exposed a decade earlier, he was, perhaps, hardly in a position to be anything *but* philosophical.

As the years passed, Martin Pattison's wealth, status, and influence grew. From their start in Minnesota's Vermilion Range, his mining interests eventually extended to Wyoming, Arizona, and even Mexico; then, as he entered his 70s, banking became the primary focus of his professional energies. He was president of the United States Bank of Superior when, at the annual Christmas dinner of the Superior Commercial Club in 1917, he announced the gift of land along the Black River that included 165-foot Big Manitou Falls—the same area he and his brother had logged in the early 1880s, and which, in 1920, would be dedicated as Wisconsin's sixth state park and named in his honor.

It was a magnificent, far-sighted gesture—but it was also a decisive response to an urgent situation. Upon learning that plans were afoot to dam the river for hydroelectricity, thereby inundating the falls, Pattison worked quickly but quietly to buy land in the area, 660 acres in all, to block the project. It seems likely that he was influenced to take this action by the example of fellow Republican Teddy Roosevelt, the first president to put conservation of natural resources on the national agenda, and it's tempting to speculate that John Muir's highly publicized—but ultimately unsuccessful—campaign to prevent the damming of the Hetch Hetchy Valley in Yosemite may have been in Pattison's mind as well.

There were personal reasons, too. As he explained to the assembled members of the Commercial Club, "In being able to grant this site to the public, I have accomplished one of my chief goals. For years I have spent much time amid the surroundings of the falls, and have received so much enjoyment there that it gradually became part of my life."

Opposite: Mahogany was the wood of choice for Fairlawn's library, which featured a fireplace of silver and Egyptian marble.

"Her crowning contribution to the cause of civic welfare was the donation, in 1920, of her former home, 'Fairlawn,' to the Children's Home and Refuge Association."

Barely one year later, Martin Pattison was dead at the age of 77. He had shown no signs of ill health until just a few days before his death, and until the end, on December 20, 1918, insisted that he'd be up and around again in short order. *The Evening Telegram* reported, "On account of his past vigor and strong constitution, it was hardly considered by those at his bedside that the earthly career of this most public spirited, generous man was about to close. He commented on simple everyday matters that he expected to attend to when the spell of weakness passed away and, turning on his pillow, went to sleep, thereby peacefully and beautifully passing out of this life into the great Beyond."

Grace Pattison, who was 62 when her husband died, did not stay long in the house they'd built together. Lois, the couple's youngest daughter and only child still living at home, suffered from rheumatoid arthritis, the symptoms of which were exacerbated by Superior's long winters and generally cool climate. Seeking the relief provided by a warmer, drier, more temperate locale, Grace and Lois moved to Los Angeles in 1920. There, Grace built a Tudor-style mansion, called Windsor, on a 37-acre estate in the Hancock Park area. She resided there until her death in 1934.

And what of Fairlawn? The genealogy Grace Pattison commissioned in the late 1920s has this to say: "In Superior, Wisconsin, which was for so long her home and with which she identified herself so closely, the name of Grace E. Pattison will be long remembered. She was in the forefront of every civic, religious, and philanthropic activity, and could be relied on for sound advice and material assistance to any enterprise which she considered for the common good ...

"Her crowning contribution to the cause of civic welfare was her donation, in 1920, of her former home, 'Fairlawn,' to the Children's Home and Refuge Association. This mansion, considered one of the most beautiful in the Northwest, she gave unreservedly to be used as a home for children ... When Mrs. Pattison no longer desired for herself such a palatial residence, she, with her customary generosity and good sense, disposed of the house in such a way that its beauties would bring happiness not to the few only, but to the many."

With the stroke of a pen, Grace Pattison transformed Fairlawn from a fairy-tale castle into a place that would tell a grittier, much less glamorous kind of story: a home for orphans and other children whose parents could not care for them. And she was so adamant that it be used for no other purpose—ever—that she made an unusual stipulation in the deed of the gift. In the event the Superior Children's Home and Refuge Association found it necessary to sell the property, "the buildings now upon said property shall be torn down."

In other words, there was to be no future for Fairlawn other than the one Grace Pattison envisioned. ✦

Chapter Three

Fairlawn
AFTER THE PATTISONS;
THE MASTER PLAN AND FUNDING FOR RESTORATION

FAIRLAWN WAS NOT THE FIRST FACILITY operated by the Superior Children's Home and Refuge Association. Since the organization's establishment in 1904—Grace Pattison was one of its founders—it had carried out its mission in a succession of buildings.

None, however, was remotely as spacious as Fairlawn. Indeed, it must have seemed positively cavernous at the time, as every stick of furniture, bolt of fabric, and *objet d'art* in the place had accompanied Grace on her move to California. (The original Pattison furnishings now on display at Fairlawn have been "repatriated" over the years by family members.) Fairlawn served as a children's home for 42 years, and in that time some 2,000 young people—babies, toddlers, school-age kids, teenagers, unwed mothers—spent portions of their lives there. This period, 1920-1962, represents the single largest "phase" of the mansion's occupancy. The writer Hugh Bishop has termed it Fairlawn's "most productive, but least romantic, period," adding, "In the hallways and rooms where the six privileged children of Martin and Grace Pattison once romped in security and opulence, dozens of less fortunate youngsters now were provided the necessities of life by the relatively meager staff and a group of volunteer workers ..."

A document prepared by the Douglas County Historical Society, "When Fairlawn was a Children's Home," outlines the basic structure of its residents' lives: "They were given a roof over their heads, a clean bed and clothes, three meals a day, haircuts, dental care, and a sense of responsibility for work and education ...

"The boys and girls who lived at Fairlawn when it was a children's home came from many diverse and tragic circumstances. Some came from large families (that were) too poor to survive, some had only one parent, some had problems at home with alcohol or abuse, some were unwed mothers. All were troubled and in need of refuge."

It may have been a spartan and regimented existence, but it was not without compensations. A number of celebrities made the long trip to Superior to visit the children, including the legendary baseball star Babe Ruth (who was himself an orphan and always had a soft spot for kids in unfortunate circumstances), comedian Bob Hope, singer/actress Doris Day, and actress Irene Dunn, best-remembered for her role as Granny on the long-running television series "The Beverly Hillbillies." Such visits were common then; children's homes occupied a more prominent place on the landscape of American life, and there were fewer charitable causes from which entertainers and athletes could choose to demonstrate their humanity.

There seems to have been a strong sense of camaraderie that bound them together, lightened their burdens, buoyed their spirits, and helped them make the best of their circumstances.

Several reunions of children's home "alumni" have been held at Fairlawn, most recently in the summer of 2000, and the memories these men and women share of their experiences are generally happy ones. At the 1995 reunion, attendees were asked to sign in on a large white crayon board where their names—along with any memories they cared to share—would be preserved for posterity. Clifford Lerand, who gave his dates of residence as 1950-56, wrote "Hey Tom, Billy & Lloyd! Remember the snow fights & licking the frosting bowls in the kitchen? And sitting under the stoves for punishment?"

There seems to have been a strong sense of camaraderie that bound them together, lightened their burdens, buoyed their spirits, and helped them make the best of their circumstances. There were opportunities for mischief, too: Also at the 1995 reunion, a man

It was a spartan and regimented existence for the children at Fairlawn, who included babies, toddlers, school-age youngsters, teens and young unwed mothers.

confessed that he was the agent behind the fire that destroyed the carriage house—it was called "the barn" then—in 1960. He'd been playing with matches, as boys will do, and things had gotten a little out of hand.

The carriage house was the last of several casualties suffered by Fairlawn during the children's home era. First to go was the conservatory, which had fallen into serious disrepair by the 1930s and was eventually razed. The iron fence that surrounded the property was taken for scrap in the 1940s to help the war effort, and circa 1952-53 the turret blew down during a severe windstorm.

Fairlawn underwent other physical changes as well. A fire escape was installed along the mansion's east elevation in the 1920s, with windows altered and doors added as necessary for access. The wooden portions of the mansion's exterior were covered with low-maintenance asbestos shingles shortly thereafter, and at some point the balustrades were removed, presumably in response to advanced deterioration. When your mission is to provide life's necessities for disadvantaged children—and your budget, obviously, is limited—the preservation of aesthetic niceties is a low priority.

Inside, the mansion's basic configuration and structure were kept remarkably intact. The large rooms of the first floor were used primarily as common areas, the second floor was the girls' dormitory, and the third floor was the boys' sleeping and living quarters. (As many as 40 young people called Fairlawn home at any given time.) A sprinkler system was installed for fire protection in the late 1940s—just in time to save the mansion when, within weeks of the installation, a blaze of unknown origin broke out in the attic. Many of the mansion's high-use spaces were eventually covered with linoleum flooring, and over the years nearly all of the lavish wall and ceiling decorations were obscured by multiple layers of paint. Happily, this fate did not befall the beautiful ornamental woodwork on the first floor, which the children were responsible for cleaning and polishing on a weekly basis.

By the early 1960s, it was apparent that Fairlawn was approaching a crossroads. With public agencies assuming more and more of the burden for the care of orphans and other needy children, the number of residents had steadily dwindled. At the same time, operation and maintenance costs were continuing to rise. In 1962, admitting that it was in an untenable position—and acknowledging the fact that it had essentially outlived its period of usefulness—the Superior Children's Home and Refuge Association decided to disband. Fairlawn's doors were closed, and, in accordance with the stipulations of Grace Pattison's will, efforts commenced to raze the mansion so that the property could be lawfully sold.

This caused no small amount of consternation among Superior's civic leaders, who recognized Fairlawn's significance not only in and of itself as a brilliant example of Victorian architecture, but also as the single most evocative symbol of that bold, big-dreaming, boomtown era when the city aspired to rival Chicago. The 20th century had not been kind to Superior: Investment had dwindled, growth had stalled, there was a sense that the city had been left behind, that the boomtown had gone bust. Duluth, in contrast, had prospered, and Superior found itself suffering from the comparison.

So it's not hard to understand why preserving Fairlawn was a priority. Scrutiny of the will by the city attorney's office revealed a loophole that had the potential to save the mansion. Should the Children's Home and Refuge Association sign off on it, the title to the property could revert to the Pattison heirs, for disposition as they saw fit.

At the same time, the venerable Douglas County Historical Society (its roots trace back to 1854) had outgrown its quarters in the former Roth home on John Avenue, where it had operated a museum since 1939, and members were considering relocating to the old

Christmas at the children's home.

armory building at John and 16th Street. But with Fairlawn vacant, there was a ground-swell of support for the idea of moving the collections and operations of the DCHS to the mansion's grandly spacious environs. Grace Pattison's heirs wholeheartedly endorsed this plan, the will was altered accordingly, and on January 2, 1963, Fairlawn became the property of the City of Superior for the price of $12,500. The DCHS, which had struck an occupancy agreement with the city, began transferring its collections that May, and on June 6, 1963, Fairlawn was officially dedicated as the Douglas County Historical Museum.

From the beginning, preservation and restoration of the mansion—which is to say, the mansion as it appeared during the Pattisons' heyday—was a priority. It was not the *only* priority, however, and it must be remembered, when considering this period of the Fairlawn story, that the mansion's primary purpose was to serve as a museum of local history. In other words, it was not *specifically* an historic house museum. While interpreting the life of Martin Pattison and the era he represented was an important aspect of its mission, the spotlight was necessarily shared with many other individuals, cultures, events, trends, and natural features that played prominent roles on the stage of regional history: Aforementioned photographer David Barry, the Ojibwe nation, and Lake Superior itself, to name but a few. The budget was shared, too, as were the resources of the DCHS, both its handful of paid staff and its legions of dedicated volunteers.

The upshot is that restoration of the mansion was, for many years, a piecemeal, stop-and-start effort—an effort characterized by the best of intentions but challenged by the dauntingly complex realm of Victorian design and decoration. A volunteer group called the Fairlawn Auxiliary worked tirelessly to restore a vestige of the mansion's splendor, holding many fund-raising events including catered dinners. Auxiliary members raised tens of thousands of dollars to replace the institutional look of the children's home with more elegant interior decorations appropriate to the turn of the century, if not entirely authentic.

A comprehensive effort to preserve the mansion began in earnest in the early 1990s,

Opposite: A meager staff and volunteer workers helped care for the children at Fairlawn for more than 40 years.

when the city, in concert with DCHS, unveiled an ambitious three-phase plan for restoring Fairlawn's exterior literally from the roof down. The point man for this effort was Marshall Weems, director of planning for the City of Superior from 1990-98. Recalls Weems, who now heads up the Housing and Redevelopment Authority for the City of St. Cloud, Minnesota, "When Herb Bergson, the mayor at the time, hired me, the city's top priorities were building a new ice arena, building a new library, and revitalizing the downtown. There wasn't much public, or political, attention being paid to Fairlawn. But the building was obviously deteriorating and in need of attention. The roof was leaking, and that dreadful asbestos siding was causing all sorts of problems. Herb Bergson recognized what a significant asset Fairlawn was to Superior, and we agreed that if we were going to preserve it, we should do the job right. A lot of things had been done over the years in the name of 'preservation,' but the proper historical context to guide these efforts was too often lacking.

"The tricky part, politically, was addressing Fairlawn's needs without jeopardizing these other, more popular, projects. We were trying to do a lot, especially for a city our size, and we had to be careful with our money. Fortunately, we were able to tap into the federal Community Development Block Grant program. Because Fairlawn was eligible for funding under the program's historic preservation provisions, we didn't have to use 'local' dollars to pay for it—which in turn freed up more money for things like the ice arena.

"Of course, when you set out to restore a Victorian mansion, you can't just go down to the Sherwin-Williams store and ask them what paint to use. I gave that assignment to Charlie Cieslak, who worked for me in the Department of Planning and Development. It wasn't the kind of thing Charlie had ever done before, but he's one of those people who's capable of doing whatever job you give him, and doing it well.

"It was Charlie who found our 'paint detective,' Bob Furhoff—an incredibly important figure in the restoration process. I like to hire people who are passionate about their work, and Bob Furhoff clearly loves what he does."

Furhoff, of Chicago, is one of the country's foremost experts on establishing the original paint colors of historic buildings. By painstakingly scraping away a century's accumulated layers of paint with a scalpel-like instrument and examining them one-by-one under a binocular microscope, he determined that Fairlawn's original exterior color scheme was a conservative palette of browns, ranging from a warm reddish tint on the first floor clapboards to more gingery hues on the upper level trims and sashes. The sole exception was the ceiling of the porch. There, Furhoff's analysis revealed that the original color was a salmony shade of pink.

"A lot of things had been done over the years in the name of 'preservation,' but the proper historical context to guide these efforts was too often lacking."

Of course, the painting had to wait until the structural elements of the project were completed. These included re-roofing; removing the asbestos siding and restoring the original scalloped cedar shakes underneath; removing a non-historic dormer thought to have been added sometime after the attic fire; installing copper gutters and downspouts; reconstructing the balustrades; and replacing some 32 storm windows with historically accurate reproductions. This last item was a particular source of pride among Superiorites, as the window frames were fashioned of redwood staves salvaged from vats that had themselves been salvaged from the long-defunct—but fondly remembered—Fitger's Brewery in Duluth. As a report prepared by DCHS at the time declared, "Fairlawn truly is recycling history."

The turret, by the way, which had gone missing since that windstorm in the early 1950s, was rebuilt in 1983. Its lines and specifications were scaled from photographs of the original. The hand that drew them belonged to a newly minted architect with a keen interest in historical preservation named James Brew. Talk about augury: In the late-1990s, Brew, a Superior resident, would serve not only as the architect of record for the most comprehensive restoration project ever undertaken at Fairlawn, but as the president of the Douglas County Historical Society.

In an attempt to beautify the Fairlawn grounds and increase their visual interest, the DCHS decided that a landscape "makeover" was in order. A plan was drawn up by a local landscape architect, and in late 1994/early 1995 Rachael Martin, the organization's executive director at the time, began contacting possible sources for the funding needed to implement this plan. One of her letters of inquiry was directed to Thomas M. Jeffris II, the president of the Jeffris Family Foundation of Janesville, Wisconsin. The Jeffris Foundation supports historic preservation in Wisconsin's smaller cities and rural areas by providing matching grants for restoration work. Some of the more notable projects the foundation has helped fund include the Frank Lloyd Wright-designed Seth Peterson Cottage on Mirror Lake near Wisconsin Dells, Villa Louis State Historic Site in Prairie du Chien, and the Stoughton Opera House.

It's rather amazing, in retrospect, to consider the effect that this letter ultimately had—like the old saying about the breeze from a butterfly's wings altering the weather half a world away. A simple request for a few bucks to help plant trees and establish flower beds precipitated a chain of events culminating in a $1.7 million restoration project—a project that involved the time and talents of dozens if not hundreds of individuals, required that the mansion be closed to the public for more than a year, and resulted in Fairlawn becoming one of the preeminent historic house museums in the Midwest.

All of this was of course unforeseeable at the time. Tom Jeffris replied to Rachael Mar-

Opposite: Work in the early 1990s returned the roof and upper floor exteriors to their original look—which helped Tom Jeffris envision the magnificent result of a full-scale restoration.

tin in a letter dated January 11, 1995, stating that landscaping was not something the foundation typically had an interest in funding. Jeffris did, however, express an interest in learning more about the property. Despite his love of old buildings in general and devotion to historic preservation in Wisconsin in particular, he'd never visited Fairlawn. Jeffris also left the door open to exploring other avenues of support more germane to the foundation's mission.

After several more rounds of correspondence, Tom Jeffris made the trans-state trip to Superior in late May. To say he was impressed by what he saw would be an understatement. It would be closer to the truth to say he was overwhelmed. (He was also a bit chagrined, as someone whose business it is to know such things, at having been unaware of the magnificence of Fairlawn.)

... the raw material Fairlawn offered to work with would, in the end, justify the investment.

Beyond what was visible to the naked eye, however, Jeffris discerned Fairlawn's *potential*—if (and it was the proverbial "big if") the proper human and financial resources could be brought to bear on a coordinated, large-scale restoration project. He knew it would be complex, he knew it would be expensive, but he was confident that the raw material Fairlawn offered to work with would, in the end, fully justify the investment. Jeffris also believed the ongoing partial restoration efforts should be halted until a comprehensive study of the mansion's current present and historic conditions could be completed. This study, undertaken literally on a room-by-room, element-by-element basis by a team of experts, would in turn guide a master plan for restoration.

"Charlie Cieslak had mentioned that there was a guy from some foundation in Janesville coming up to look at Fairlawn," recalls Marshall Weems, "and that maybe I'd want to come over and meet him. My schedule was pretty tight that day, but I managed to get to Fairlawn just as Charlie, Rachael Martin, and James Brew were sitting down with Tom Jeffris. He didn't say much until, during a discussion of the ongoing exterior restoration, Charlie dropped Bob Furhoff's name. Tom really perked up at that. He was well aware of Furhoff's reputation, and I think that helped convince him that we were serious about doing things right.

"Of course," Weems adds, "Tom could also see that we needed a lot of help."

On June 5, after returning to Janesville, Jeffris wrote Rachael Martin to express his enthusiasm for Fairlawn—and to stress the importance of completing a comprehensive study/master plan as soon as possible. He offered to help finance this effort through the foundation, suggesting renowned preservation architect David Evans, a principal in Quinn Evans/Architects of Ann Arbor, Michigan, as the person to head it up. Jeffris knew Evans personally through their mutual involvement in the Villa Louis project, a commission Evans had earned by dint of his award-winning work on such high-profile restorations as the Old Executive Office Building in Washington, D.C., the Thomas Jefferson and John Adams buildings of the Library of Congress, and the Wayne County Courthouse in Detroit.

The idea of a master plan for Fairlawn, coupled with Jeffris' offer of financial assistance, galvanized not only Marshall Weems, but also Margaret Ciccone, Superior's mayor from 1995 until mid-2000. Weems and Ciccone promoted the project tirelessly among civic leaders and the community at large, having grasped early on the enormous significance it could have in Superior.

Weems, in particular, worked closely with the Jeffris Foundation to secure grant moneys and assemble the overall funding package for the project. "Tom Jeffris was quick to pick up on the fact that we were well-meaning but lacked direction," he notes. "That's why the study was so important: It gave us a soundly reasoned blueprint, and it was assembled by the best people we could have possibly had—people we never would have found if it weren't for Tom Jeffris. Meeting Tom was such an unbelievable break for us. As I've often said, what he and the Jeffris Foundation really gave Superior was an opportunity to dream."

In October, city and DCHS officials traveled to Milwaukee to attend the annual board meeting of the Jeffris Foundation to discuss the study/master plan grant. Architect David Evans had already visited Fairlawn by that time, and his preliminary assessment underscored the need to refrain from further work at the mansion until the study could be accomplished and the master plan finalized. By then, too, Gail Caskey Winkler of LCA Associates in Philadelphia had been brought in. One of the country's foremost authorities on Victorian design and the author of several standard references on the subject, Winkler had collaborated with Evans on the master plan for Villa Louis. Respectful of each other's expertise and with a proven track record as partners, Evans and Winkler were the obvious choices to tackle Fairlawn.

On March 25, 1996, after several months of active behind-the-scenes organizing, the DCHS held a press conference to announce that it had received a "major preservation grant" from the Jeffris Family Foundation. This grant, in the amount of $30,000, was to be matched by $15,000 from DCHS and $15,000 from the Tourism Development Foundation of the Superior/Douglas County Chamber of Commerce. The $60,000 total would underwrite the costs of developing a master plan for restoration. David Evans and his staff at Quinn Evans would handle the architectural/structural aspects of the plan, while LCA Associates led by Gail Winkler with Roger W. Moss would be responsible for its decorative arts component. Shawn Graff, president of Graff & Associates, a museum/historic preservation consulting firm based in Hartford, Wisconsin, was retained to provide project coordination and oversee preparation of the final report. Graff was also charged with developing an operations plan to usher Fairlawn and DCHS into the 21st century.

Site visits by members of the planning team commenced shortly thereafter, and throughout the summer of 1996 a veritable blizzard of correspondence—letters, faxes, phone calls—flew back and forth among the major players, Rachael Martin of DCHS, and Superior city officials. There were innumerable questions that needed to be asked and answered, countless pieces of information that needed to be ferreted out and delivered to the proper hands. During this period, too, contact was initiated with two state agencies with which the master plan would eventually have to pass muster. One was the State Historical Society of Wisconsin. The other was DILHR, the Wisconsin Department of Industry, Labor, and Human Relations (now subsumed under the state Department of Commerce).

Because Fairlawn is listed on the National Register of Historic Places—it was so designated in 1981—the State Historical Society must review and approve any construction plans prior to their implementation. The purpose here is to ensure that the building's authenticity and historical integrity—indeed, the very qualities that make it historically significant—are not compromised. And because Fairlawn is a public space, it is subject to state fire and safety regulations, as well as to the accessibility provisions of the Americans with Disabilities Act—compliance with which fell, at the time, under the aegis of DILHR. (At the outset of the planning process, Fairlawn was still technically considered a children's home. Much of the give-and-take with DILHR centered on the changes necessary for reclassification as a museum.) Reconciling the State Historical Society's concerns with the mandates of DILHR was not always an easy task, but the various parties seem to have recognized the significance of the project and the importance of getting Fairlawn "up to code." As a result, there was a great deal of cooperation and, for the most part, precious little contentiousness.

In late July 1996, a preliminary draft of the master plan was submitted to DCHS, the

City of Superior, and other parties for review and comment. From that point on, the review and comment process was essentially continuous, serving to polish the plan's content and refine its objectives until the final document, dated October 5, 1996, was unveiled. While the plan addressed *everything*, from such pressing needs as shoring up the mansion's foundation to such long-range dreams as rebuilding the vanished conservatory and carriage house, its main thrust was three-pronged: Completion of the exterior restoration (primarily the first floor), interior and exterior modifications as necessary to ensure code compliance, and restoration of the prominent interior spaces of the first floor to match as accurately as possible their appearance during the mid-1890s, i.e. the aesthetic apotheosis of Pattison occupancy.

This "Phase I" project, as it was termed, carried an estimated price tag of $1.35 million—a level that had already been deemed feasible by the entities who would eventually pay the bill. It reflected an anticipated $600,000 challenge grant from the Jeffris Family Foundation, $150,000 apiece from the coffers of Douglas County and the City of Superior, and the remainder, $450,000, generated by a massive DCHS-led fund-raising drive. These numbers had been hammered out in discussions involving all the project partners. Yet the most intensive negotiations had been those between the Jeffris Foundation and the City of Superior.

Because DCHS had never mounted a fund-raising campaign of this magnitude, there was concern in both Janesville and Superior about a potential shortfall in the local match. The foundation's contribution of approximately 44.5 percent of the project cost represented a substantial increase over its typical grant of one-third of the total amount, and Tom Jeffris, while unflagging in his enthusiasm to restore Fairlawn, was not about to sign any checks until he was convinced that the matching funds could be generated and the project completed as planned. He and the foundation had suffered what Jeffris termed a "major disaster" on an earlier project when a local partner failed to meet its financial obligation.

In fact, it looked for a time as if the master plan for Fairlawn might end up as just another elaborate document gathering dust on a shelf. "The project was dead in the water," Tom Jeffris candidly acknowledges. Fortunately, Margaret Ciccone, Marshall Weems, and a core group of like-minded individuals on the Superior City Council understood what was at stake—what Superior stood to gain if the project came to pass, and what it stood to lose if it did not. They joined forces to push through a unique resolution, a resolution giving the City of Superior the authority to *guarantee* not only the $150,000 share originally apportioned to it, but the $450,000 apportioned to DCHS as well. In other words, if the DCHS fund-raising campaign fell short of its goal, the city would kick in the rest of the money.

Marshall Weems traveled to Janesville to make this pitch to the Jeffris Foundation in person—and, by so doing, to demonstrate the City of Superior's commitment to the Fairlawn project. According to Weems, "We wanted Tom and his board members, Henry Fuldner and Chuck Rydberg, to know how serious we were." His appearance—and the offer he put on the table—had the intended effect. Tom Jeffris was bowled over. To this day, he refers to the City of Superior as "a class act," and to Weems and Ciccone as "two of the finest local officials the foundation has ever worked with."

For her part, Margaret Ciccone recalls, "We were fortunate, at the time, to have some very progressive people on the City Council—people who shared a vision for Superior's future. That's what our guarantee of funding for Fairlawn really boiled down to: An investment in the future of our community. Over the years, Superiorites have developed a tendency to focus on what's wrong with their city. By restoring Fairlawn, we hoped to reestablish a link to our history, instill a sense of community pride, and get people to focus on what's right about Superior."

Toward this end, on October 1, 1996, the Superior City Council adopted a resolution, introduced by Mayor Ciccone, designating the restoration of the Fairlawn Mansion as the "official sesquicentennial project" for the City of Superior. As the project was expected to take at least a year from beginning to end—and as work was expected to begin sometime in mid-1997—its completion would coincide with the State of Wisconsin's sesquicentennial celebration in 1998. (The vote, by the way, was unanimous.)

There was one unfinished item of business, however. Although Gail Winkler had catalogued most of the decorative aspects of Fairlawn's first floor and made recommendations for their restoration, a detailed investigation of the Pattison-era wall and ceiling treatments remained to be undertaken. Using a special light, Winkler and Roger Moss could tell there were elements of decoration—which, in fact, were visible in the Barry and Greenfield photographs—that had been obscured by subsequent painting and plastering. This investigation called for a specialist in paint microscopy, the removal and analysis of one microscopically thin layer of paint after another until the desired surface is revealed. It is something like a hybrid of neurosurgery and archaeology—and there was no one better qualified for the task than Robert Furhoff, the same man who had documented Fairlawn's original exterior paint scheme several years earlier.

Furhoff estimated the cost of the job at $47,000, and Tom Jeffris, keenly aware of how crucial his findings would be in terms of restoring the interior to its brimming historical splendor, unhesitatingly agreed to add the entire amount on top of the $600,000 already promised by the foundation. On November 4, 1996, a press release from the Office of the May-or of the City of Superior announced the receipt of a $600,000 challenge grant from the Jeffris Family Foundation, a grant that would provide matching funds for a $1.4 million restoration of the Fairlawn Mansion. In Mayor Ciccone's words, "The extraordinary generosity of the Jeffris Family Foundation and the direct involvement of the foundation's president, Tom Jeffris, will enrich our community forever."

Jeffris himself added, "I am happy that our foundation can be the catalyst for the restoration project. We can return Fairlawn to its original glory." ✦

FAIRLAWN

Chapter Four

Restoration Begins

WITH THE MASTER PLAN IN HAND and the funding in place, the next step in the Fairlawn restoration process was to prepare the "construction documents"—the detailed, item-by-item specifications of the architectural/structural work to be completed. These documents would, in turn, be made available to any qualified contractors interested in bidding on the job. It was at this point that James Brew of Duluth-based LHB Engineers & Architects was retained as the architect of record for the project. Brew's professional knowledge of Fairlawn (you'll recall that he had designed the replacement turret in the early '80s), along with his personal interest in the property as a Douglas County Historical Society board member, made him an ideal choice. Working closely with the staff of Quinn Evans, Brew spent much of the first half of 1997 on this task.

Two of the more prominent components of this overall "blueprint" included modification of the porte-cochere entrance on the mansion's west side to provide "barrier-free" access (that is, a wheelchair ramp), and provision of a similarly barrier-free restroom on the mansion's first floor. Both of these items had been identified in the master plan as necessary for compliance with ADA regulations. But the single largest and most difficult element, also necessary for getting Fairlawn "up to code," was the construction of a fully enclosed, fire-rated stairwell on the south (back) side of the building. Quinn Evans had drawn up several alternative versions of how this stairwell might be constructed, all based on the idea of using interior spaces—the servants' stairway and butler's pantry, for example—deemed unsuitable or of very low priority for restoration. The advantage of such an approach is that it would leave the mansion's exterior unaltered—a major "selling point" in terms of obtaining the blessing of the State Historical Society.

Not everyone close to the project was convinced that this approach was appropriate. One such critic was Jim Pellman, a long-time DCHS board member who over the years had donated hundreds of hours to various Fairlawn-related activities. Pellman believed that, although their appearance had been altered since the Pattisons' tenure, the "historical truth" represented by the spaces scheduled to be sacrificed for the new

The turret, which had blown down in a 1950s windstorm, was replaced in 1983. Architect James Brew designed the new one using photographs of the original.

fire exit remained intact. He argued that an important element of the Fairlawn story would be permanently lost if these rooms—rooms that had been the heart and soul of the living, breathing Pattison household—were given up.

Pellman's impassioned but well-reasoned argument struck a resonant chord with James Brew. In designing new construction for historic buildings, Brew has always advocated the notion of "reversibility," i.e., the ability to "undo" the new construction if necessary and return the building to its prior condition. The fire exit proposals put on the table by Quinn Evans failed this test, so Brew encouraged them to rethink their approach and explore alternatives that would not compromise the mansion's existing interior rooms. Quinn Evans' creative response was to attach the fire exit to the exterior of Fairlawn's south elevation and enclose it in such a way that it would appear seamlessly integral with the rest of the structure—or at least it would appear that way to all but the tiny minority of observers schooled in the nuances of Victorian architecture.

"A person who really knows Victorian architecture can look at this and tell it's not original," notes Brew. "I think that's why the State Historical Society approved it. They're very insistent that new construction on historic buildings isn't 'passed off' as original, and although most people can't tell that the fire tower's an 'add-on' because of the way the exterior finishes match the rest of the house, a trained eye is still able to discern the difference.

"And," Brew stresses, "it's *reversible*. If something changes in the future and it becomes necessary to remove the fire tower, it would be fairly simple to take it down and restore the exterior to its original appearance. That wasn't the case with the earlier designs."

As desirable as this revision proved, however, it had the effect of ratcheting up the overall project cost. Indeed, as early as March, 1997, when Brew and Quinn Evans were in the thick of defining the scope of work to be accomplished, David Evans expressed concern that the costs of code-related construction and structural repairs had risen beyond what had been budgeted in the grant proposal—the upshot being that the money might run out before the restoration of the interior could be completed. This necessitated an almost continuous process of revising the scope of work in order to get the maximum bang for the buck, subject to the guiding principle that it was preferable to restore a few high-priority spaces comprehensively and without compromise than to do a partial and incomplete job on a lot of them.

On September 4, 1997, restoration commenced on the grandest, most ambitious project in Fairlawn's history.

The construction documents were finished in July, with bids from interested contractors due by early August. J.R. Jensen & Son, Inc., of Superior, won the bid. The Jensen firm was well-acquainted with Fairlawn, having served as the general contractor for the first phase of the exterior restoration that took place in the early 1990s. On September 4, 1997, restoration commenced on the grandest, most ambitious project in Fairlawn's history. By then, DCHS had already closed the mansion to the public and moved its operations and exhibits to a leased space in Superior's Mariner Mall, thereby allowing the work to proceed in as unimpeded a fashion as possible.

The presumption, at the time the move was made, was that it was temporary and that DCHS would reoccupy Fairlawn at the conclusion of the restoration, sometime in the fall of 1998. This did not come to pass, however. In addition to Fairlawn, the City of Superior owns two other historic properties operated as museums: the Old Fire House and Police Museum, built as a fire hall in 1897-98, and the *S.S. Meteor* Whaleback Ship and Muse-

Page 62: Restoration commenced with the removal of the back porch, foundation repair, and the construction of a wheelchair ramp on the west side.

Fairlawn's exterior was the focus of restoration attention in 1997, because winter was just around the corner.

um, the *Meteor* being the last of the "whaleback" freighters, built in Superior in the 1890s, that plied the Great Lakes during the first half of the 20th century. Unlike Fairlawn, the operation of which was contracted to DCHS by the city (thus enabling the retention of paid professional staff), the other museums were run solely by volunteers under the direction of the Superior/Douglas County Chamber of Commerce. These properties received no city funding, and in fact the Chamber's support was based primarily on goodwill and a "handshake" agreement with the city.

With Mayor Ciccone in the vanguard, the City of Superior began taking steps to bring all three museums into a single fold. There were serious maintenance issues confronting the Old Fire House and *Meteor* museums that needed to be addressed. Also, the ongoing, large-scale restoration of Fairlawn meant that its role would soon change, and that instead of being both a local history museum and an historic house museum, it would be primarily—if not exclusively—the latter. A group known as the Heritage Committee, with representation from the city, the county, the Chamber of Commerce, DCHS, the three museums, and the public, was convened to explore alternatives for consolidating—and thereby improving—the management of these historic sites. Shawn Graff of Graff & Associates, who earlier had coordinated the development of the master plan for Fairlawn,

Above: Sagging foundation areas were restored with a raised bead of mortar between the stones, in keeping with the original look.

Opposite: The exterior fire escape on the east side of the mansion was removed and an enclosed fire exit stairwell was built on the south side.

was retained to advise the committee on exactly what these alternatives might be and how they might work.

In August 1998, the Heritage Committee evaluated the options presented by Graff and concluded that the formation of a new "umbrella" entity to operate all three museums was the best approach. This decision was not met with universal enthusiasm, however, especially within DCHS. With the creation of this new organization to manage Fairlawn, DCHS would in effect be dispossessed, losing both its "home" and the city funding that was its lifeline. A series of heated exchanges ensued, the climate grew rancorous, and even now there remains resentment among some DCHS members over the outcome. But on November 17, 1998, the Superior City Council adopted a resolution establishing the Superior Public Museum Board for the purpose of overseeing the management of the three historic properties. An offshoot of this board—its "professional" branch, so to speak—known as Superior Public Museums, Inc., was created to handle the museums' day-to-day operations.

DCHS no longer has an organizational presence at Fairlawn. It now occupies a suite of rooms in the basement of the Old Superior Post Office, a downtown building recently renovated and refurbished for use as office and retail space.

Fairlawn's exterior was the focus of restoration attention in 1997, not only because it made sense in terms of the logical sequence of construction but also because winter was just around the corner—and no one wants to be working outside during winter in Superior, Wisconsin. Brew and Charlie Cieslak, who had been charged with overseeing the project for the City of Superior, were on the site almost daily to monitor progress, put out "fires," ensure quality control, and respond to the myriad questions and problems that were bound to arise (and did).

For example, the mansion's brownstone foundation, which was sagging badly on the north and west sides, had to be excavated, shored up with concrete blocks and steel gird-

Opposite: Once the asbestos siding was removed, workmen set about repairing the wooden boards underneath, here on the rear porch.

ers, and then refaced above grade with matching stone. During the final stages of this process, Brew noticed that the masons were leaving a concave groove in the mortar between the stones. This is common practice in contemporary construction—but in Martin Pattison's time masons finished joints with a raised bead, not a recessed one. Brew's insistence that the masons hew to the historically accurate method, which meant that they'd have to redo a significant portion of the foundation, occasioned more than a little grumbling. By the time they had finished, however, they were converts. As Cieslak recalls, "When they had the chance to stand back and look at what they'd done, I think they were pretty proud of their work."

Another item Brew insisted upon—although, again, it jacked up the bottom line—

Brew insisted that the masons hew to the historically accurate method, which meant that they'd have to redo a significant portion of the foundation.

Opposite: Workmen faced many daunting projects when they began the restoration of Fairlawn, from repairing foundation deterioration to re-creating the ornate capitals that crowned the porch columns.

was the use of opaque "spandrel" glass in the windows cut into the front porch foundation. It would have been cheaper simply to cover the openings with plywood panels and paint them black (clear glazing was not an option for a variety of reasons), but Brew wanted spandrel because it is more aesthetically pleasing. By day, especially, it reflects light in such a way as to be indistinguishable from the mansion's other fenestration.

The enclosed stairwell on the south elevation was another of the first items tackled by the construction crew—along with the removal of the old, rickety, *a lá* urban tenement fire escape on the east side. A crane was brought in to handle this task, and on the appoint-

ed day the loosened stairs were clean-and-jerked from the side of the building in one fell swoop. The new "tower" on the south side went up quickly. One of the more interesting aspects of its construction was the use of a man-made product, "artstone," to match the native brownstone in the original foundation. Amazing as it may seem, given the abundance of this distinctive reddish sandstone in the Lake Superior region (and its prevalence in buildings of Fairlawn's vintage), it is no longer being quarried—thus the necessity of substituting artstone, a composite formed of sand and cement that closely duplicates the color, texture, and surface contour of the real thing.

Man-made materials were also employed to duplicate the ornate capitals that crown the porch columns. These were originally made of two blocks of solid wood, joined and carved in deep relief by master artisans. Only one of these blocks (one half of a complete capital) survived. When it was discovered adjacent to the porte-cochere entrance, a plaster mold of it was made that, in turn, became the basis for new capitals—dead ringers—cast out of a long-lasting wood-fiber composite. The porch columns themselves, solid wood originally, were replaced by steel beams. To preserve the appropriate aesthetic effect, these beams were concealed within grooved wooden veneers.

Repainting the first-floor clapboards to match the color specifications supplied by

Opposite and above: Exquisite details on Fairlawn's exterior include "fish-scale" shakes, curved lintels and carved balustrades.

Robert Furhoff was on the agenda at this time as well. After several methods of preparing the surface were tried and rejected, the paint contractor struck gold with an innovative blasting technique using shredded cornhusks. The husks contained just enough abrasive content to gently erode the old paint and reveal the bare wood, while removing as little of it as possible.

While the exterior work was going on, Furhoff himself was busily exposing the various surfaces of Fairlawn's interior.

While this exterior work was going on, Furhoff himself was busily exposing the various surfaces of Fairlawn's interior—ceilings, moldings, walls, etc.—and documenting their original motifs and colors. He was guided in his investigations by the Barry and Greenfield photographs, which told him where to look and what to look for. It was a slow, painstaking process, at times requiring him to remove layers of paint that were little more than films of colored dust. But his skill and persistence paid off, combining to uncover a higher level of detail and artistry than the photographs indicated—more, in fact, than anyone had bargained for when the budget for the grant was hammered out.

For this and other reasons, including the discovery that the foundation was in a more advanced state of disrepair than anyone suspected, it was clear within a month of the project's inception that completing the restoration as planned was going to require an additional infusion of capital. (Indeed, the contingency funds built into the original budget

had already been gobbled up.) Marshall Weems crunched the numbers, with input from David Evans and Gail Winkler, and determined that an extra $200,000 would be sufficient to ensure that all the decorative elements specified in the master plan—the decorative painting in particular—would be completed in full.

Above: Artisans worked with stencils to paint many of the repeated patterns on ceilings.

Opposite: Trim was painstakingly restored and plaster repaired on walls and ceilings.

Tom Jeffris, who appreciatively credits Weems with keeping him updated regularly on developments at Fairlawn, was apprised of the anticipated budget shortfall. Once again he stepped up to the plate with an offer of financial assistance. Jeffris is well-known in the historic restoration community for his insistence on the best of everything in the projects the foundation helps underwrite. This, coupled with his enthusiasm for Fairlawn and his faith in the "team" that had been assembled, made the decision to kick in another $100,000 relatively easy. The City of Superior did its part as well, guaranteeing the $100,000 local match. On November 13, 1997, receipt of the grant, the third awarded to Superior by the Jeffris Foundation, was announced in a news release from Mayor Ciccone's office. This brought the total amount of funding for the project to approximately $1.6 million.

With the onset of winter, attention turned to Fairlawn's interior. Much of this work was decidedly not glamorous: Peeling off yellowed linoleum flooring and refinishing the hard maple boards underneath; patching cracked plaster and installing new walls and ceilings as necessary; cleaning and revarnishing woodwork; and replacing various pieces of

molding that had been lost or damaged over the years. All were tedious but necessary steps that underpin all restoration projects. New furnace boilers, specified by state regulators for code compliance, were installed during this period as well.

While removing the antiquated, exposed fire suppression sprinklers and replacing them with a more modern and less obtrusive system, workmen discovered an alarming hodge-podge of electrical wiring behind the ceilings, some of which dated to the earliest days of the mansion. Because there would never be a better opportunity to head off this accident waiting to happen, the City of Superior authorized an additional $50,000 from its own coffers for new electrical work. Opening the ceilings—down to the laths, in most cases—also allowed workmen to trace the old gas lines and pinpoint the locations of the original light fixtures.

No ceilings or walls were removed, of course, until Robert Furhoff had had an opportunity to expose a portion of their surfaces and document the original colors and design motifs. "Each room had different conditions for restoration," he says. "In the parlor and main hallway, for example, we were pretty much able to replicate everything as it was originally. In the library and dining room, there were some aspects that we were able to replicate, while others had to be interpreted, based on fragmentary evidence and what could be gleaned from the photographs. Unfortunately, the decorative painting in the music room was totally lost, so in that case there was no choice but to do an interpretive restoration."

Charlie Cieslak, who watched Furhoff at work many times over the course of Fairlawn's various restorations (which began with him standing in the basket of a "cherry picker" to take paint samples from the third floor), marvels at his expertise. "Furhoff's one of the most amazing guys I've ever seen," declares Cieslak.

For his part, Furhoff deflects praise. "My job," he shrugs, "is mostly boring technical stuff. I just specify the colors and make drawings of the patterns I find—the artists do the rest."

To keep the public's interest in Fairlawn piqued during the construction process, the

Opposite: "Paint detective" Robert Furhoff carefully scraped many layers of paint to determine the original colors, including those of the wallpaper and decorative stenciling.

DCHS scheduled monthly "hard hat" tours during the winter and spring of 1998, enabling visitors to see for themselves the work that was being performed. A news release announcing the April hard hat tour offered a rundown of what to expect: "Visitors will see the progress made since last month, including the handicapped ramp nearing completion, the new fire exit tower, the columns on the front porch, and the new stairs added to the front.

DCHS scheduled monthly "hard hat" tours during the winter and spring of 1998, enabling visitors to see for themselves the work that was being performed.

Top photos opposite: In addition to plaster and lath repair, wood newel post caps were re-created based on one found in storage.

"On the inside, the new ceilings in the hallways, library, sitting room, parlor, music room, dining room, and stair landing are completed. The sprinkler system has been recessed with new sprinkler heads.

"The frieze areas of the sitting room, parlor, and main hallway show the decorative painting to be replicated when the artists begin this spring.

"Visitors will also notice the locations of the antique chandeliers to be installed, the repair of the tiles in the vestibules and on the first-floor landing, and learn about the carpeting being made for each room.

Bottom photos opposite: New capitals for columns were cast using a mold of the half of an original capital discovered still in use in Fairlawn. The new capitals were cast out of a wood-fiber composite.

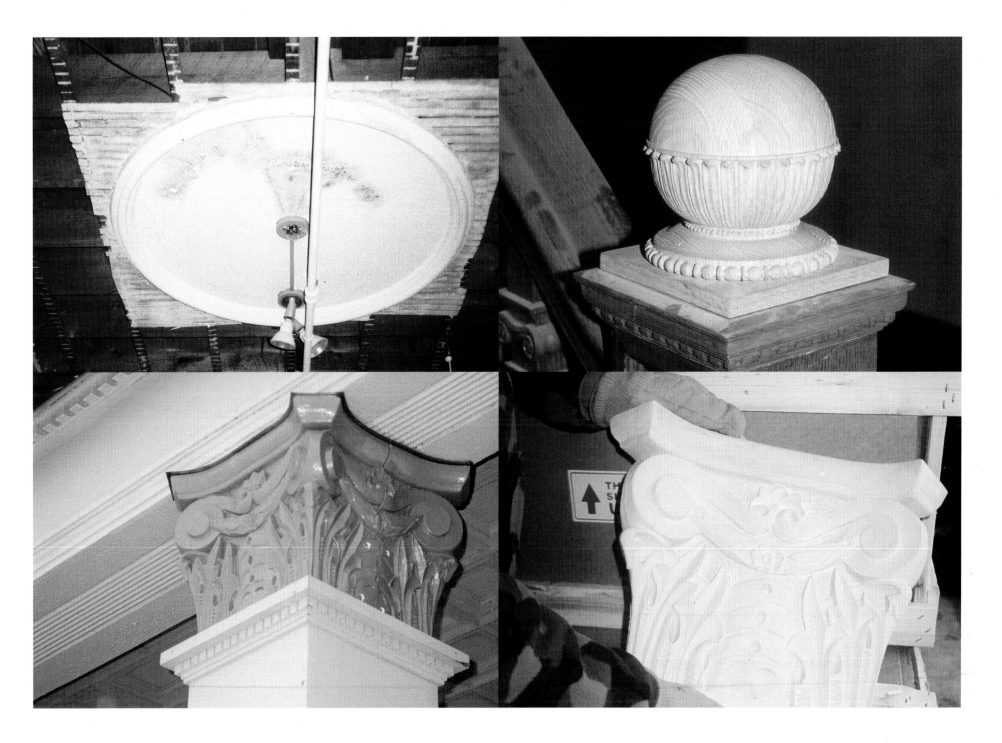

"The tour includes viewing the inside of the newly completed fire exit tower, and the handicapped bathroom still in progress. Visitors will also view Mr. Pattison's office, where an original decorative hand-painted ceiling was recently discovered."

The discovery of this ceiling, which was revealed when workmen removed a non-historic "dropped" ceiling, was perhaps the most exciting "find" of the entire restoration. An ethereal, almost Edenesque scene of blue sky and wispy clouds, it is a dazzling example of *trompe l'oeil* ("fool the eye") painting—and a tribute to the artistry of the unknown hand that created it. It is not much of a leap to suppose that this imaginary vault of sky helped transport Martin Pattison to the wild, unspoiled places to which he was drawn so irresistibly.

This discovery did, however, force a slight change in plans, as what had been assumed to be a matter of historic *restoration* had suddenly become a matter of historic *preservation*. Work was halted and, for now, the non-ceiling portions of Pattison's office remain essentially as they were when the ceiling was uncovered. A portion of the proceeds from this book, in fact, have been earmarked for the room's eventual completion.

A major player in the Fairlawn project bowed out that same spring when Marshall Weems, who had championed the restoration from the very beginning and been the point man in negotiating with the Jeffris Foundation and putting the overall funding package together, left Superior to head up the St. Cloud, Minnesota, Housing and Redevelopment Authority. He had not only done his part, he had done it with great energy, great professionalism, and great equanimity. Everyone close to the project agrees that it never would have happened without Weems' quietly effective leadership.

In May 1998, a team from Affiliated Artists in Greendale, Wisconsin, arrived in Superior to carry out the painting of Fairlawn's walls and ceilings according to Furhoff's specifications—specifications so rigorously intricate and technically demanding that only one other firm even bothered to bid on the job. The most anticipated portion of the entire project, the restoration of the mansion's exquisite decorative elements, had officially begun. ◆

Opposite: Workmen removed a dropped ceiling in Martin Pattison's office to discover a decorative hand-painted ceiling. Its center is an ethereal scene of blue sky and wispy clouds—what's called a *trompe l'oeil* ("fool the eye") painting (bottom right).

Chapter Five

The Splendor Restored

ESTABLISHED IN 1993, Affiliated Artists is a relatively young company. Its three founding partners, however, boast some 60 years' combined experience in reproducing "lost" surface treatments, creating new designs appropriate to older buildings, and providing original finishes for contemporary spaces such as the Marcus Center for the Performing Arts in Milwaukee. From restoring turn-of-the-century theaters in the Upper Peninsula of Michigan to re-creating Frank Lloyd Wright's designs at Roosevelt University in Chicago, their resume is notable for the range of decorative and architectural styles in encompasses.

"We take on any job that piques our interest and pays the bills," quips partner David Strickland, who served as Affiliated Artists' on-site project manager at Fairlawn.

And while historic homes are a staple—the Pabst Mansion in Milwaukee; Hearthstone in Appleton, Wisconsin; and the Adams House in Deadwood, South Dakota, are some to which they've lent their talents—perhaps the largest component of their business, says Strickland, is churches. To cite just one example, they created a Celtic decorative scheme as part of the restoration of the Old St. Patrick's Church in downtown Chicago, a church that pre-dates the 1871 fire.

"Churches are very spiritual spaces anyway," notes Strickland, "and because we're often the only people in the building, this feeling of spirituality is intensified. Most churches were highly decorated, so it's extremely satisfying to return them back to the way they looked originally."

Working closely with Robert Furhoff as well as with contractor J.R. Jensen's crew of carpenters, plasterers, and drywall installers, the Affiliated Artists team shuttled between Greendale (a Milwaukee suburb) and Superior until October. Led by Strickland, a team of two or three artists would spend from two to three weeks at a stretch at Fairlawn, working room by room through the six targeted for restoration. The "order of battle" began with the main hallway, followed by the library, sitting room, dining room, and parlor, concluding with the music room. When the artists were finished with a room, they would return to the Milwaukee area—and their studio/workshop—to prepare for the next "assault." This also gave the team an opportunity to consult with Furhoff, who by then was back in his own studio in Chicago.

The fact that each room took a minimum of two weeks to complete provides an indication not only of the delicate and complex nature of the task, but of the level of artistry brought to bear on it. As noted previously, each room presented somewhat different conditions for restoration, based on what Furhoff was—or was not—able to determine in the course of his investigations. In the rooms in which he could document all or a portion of the original designs, Affiliated Artists used his drawings—Strickland likens them to "blueprints with color codes"—to create Mylar stencils. These stencils, in turn, facilitated the duplication of motifs that occurred in repeating patterns on the ceiling borders and decorative friezes. Elsewhere, they reproduced the designs "freehand," just as those unknown painters of the 1890s had created them.

"The crowning jewel of the mansion" is how Fairlawn's decorative painting was described in a 1999 episode of the popular Arts & Entertainment Network television series "America's Castles." The segment, entitled "Castles of the Lumber Barons," went on to note that Martin Pattison hired "fine painters to create exquisite freehand works of art that adorned many of the ceilings and walls of Fairlawn."

"When you're duplicating the same brush strokes those old-timers made," muses Strickland, "you can almost feel them looking over your shoulder. It makes you appreciate their skill all the more."

These same basic techniques—stenciling and freehand painting—were also used in the areas where interpretive re-creation, rather than strict replication, was called for. Strickland estimates that the split between the two techniques was "about 50-50." All of this work was preceded by studio renderings of the designs to be reproduced, some highly detailed and worked out very completely, others looser and more impressionistic.

There was something of a crisis early on, when the painters complained that the existing plaster surface was too "grainy" and would compromise the subtle effects they sought to create. The on-site brain trust, including James Brew and Charlie Cieslak, put their

Page 84: The library ceiling.

Opposite: Artisans from Affiliated Artists in Greendale, Wisconsin, tackled the demanding and precise work of rolling on ceiling stencil patterns, here in the main hall.

heads together and found a solution in a product called Glidwall. Then manufactured by the Glidden Paint Co., Glidwall is an extremely thin sheet of fiberglass-reinforced polyester that is applied in much the same manner as wallpaper, bonding to the underlying plaster and providing a finely textured surface for painting. The addition of this "skim coat" required a $15,000 change order to the construction specifications, but there is universal agreement that it was money well spent.

On the dining room ceiling, which is coffered into four quadrants surrounding a center oval, the painting was not done directly on the surface itself, but on individual canvas panels. This work was accomplished in the Greendale studio. Then, the completed panels were transported to Fairlawn and affixed to the ceiling. While this may sound innovative, it is in fact a technique that was historically very common in buildings of Fairlawn's scale and opulence.

Not all of the work performed by Affiliated Artists involved painting. In the parlor, the artists spent days meticulously gilding the ornamental moldings of the mantelpiece, as well as the lintels of the windows and doorways and the capitals of the pilasters that flank them, with 24-karat gold leaf.

Although absolute "line accuracy" was not always possible, the artists were keenly attuned to what Furhoff calls "the rhythm and pattern" of the original motifs. These were, for the most part, variations of the rinceau style, which features gracefully intertwined vines, flowers, and other foliage. The discovery of the intact ceiling painting in Martin Pattison's office also provided them with a clearer understanding of the aesthetic sensibility that prevailed at the time of Fairlawn's construction as well as the sophistication of the original artists.

"It really gave us a feel for the style, the technique, and especially the subtlety of the original painting," notes Strickland. "We couldn't get that from the exposures Bob made. They gave us the basic colors and patterns, but that was all. Once we saw the office ceiling, we

Art conservator Ron Koenig of Lansing, Michigan, led the exacting preservation of the office ceiling, which included plaster repair and a re-creation of a section of the original painting that had been damaged.

Above: Stencils were used for the patterns on the main hall ceiling.

Opposite: All the music room painting was done freehand

by the painters from Affiliated Artists, including the

detailed depictions of instruments.

could focus on capturing that same subtlety and expressiveness in the rest of the house."

The music room is a brilliant example of success in meeting this goal. With the original designs entirely lost, the artists had nothing to go on except the little that could be inferred from the Barry and Greenfield photographs. By saving this room for last, however, the experience and insight they had gained enabled them to create a scheme, keeping to the rinceau style, that satisfies all the relevant historical criteria, but more importantly is fresh, spontaneous, and utterly faithful to the spirit of the mansion. The medallions of musical instruments—a quartet of them—that adorn the cornice frieze contribute an especially delightful note. As an aside, Robert Furhoff was so confident in the artists' abilities by this point that he gave them no direction whatsoever. Instead, he simply turned them loose, allowing them to flex their creative muscles.

"By the time we got to the music room," allows Strickland, "we didn't have to do much preliminary drawing at all. The designs were mostly in our heads, and they went from there straight to the plaster.

"From a technical standpoint," he concludes, "there was nothing we did at Fairlawn that we don't do on a regular basis. What made the job unusual was its size, and the fact that each room had a completely different scheme. But that's what made it fun. There was a tremendous feeling of satisfaction when we came down from the scaffolding after finishing a room and saw the way it all came together."

Meanwhile, Gail Winkler was busily mobilizing the international network of suppliers she has cultivated as a preeminent authority on Victorian design and decoration. Some of these sources are so singular in terms of the products or services they provide (and their level of quality) that Winkler refuses to divulge their identities—which is to say, she does not want her competitors, such as they are, to know about them.

Because the selection of carpets, draperies, and other textiles had to wait until Furhoff had established the colors predominant in each room, one of the first things Winkler

turned her attention to was lighting. Only two light fixtures original to the rooms targeted for restoration remained: A wrought iron, swirled-glass lantern that had originally hung in the vestibule but had at some point been moved to the main hall, and another lantern-style fixture at the rear of the main hall near the porte-cochere entrance. This latter piece was missing its two "arms," but was in sufficiently good condition to warrant repair, using the old photographs to replicate the arms.

There were three other fixtures in place, however, that while not original to Fairlawn were of the correct vintage, style, and quality to admirably serve the purposes of the restoration. These pieces, all combination gas-electric chandeliers, hung in the library, sitting room, and parlor, and Winkler was satisfied that with minor adjustments—lowering their height and installing reproduction carbon-filament bulbs that emit what she describes as "a mellow, golden light"—they could stay where they were. In 1994, former DCHS Executive Director Rachael Martin had been able to purchase these fixtures, which decades earlier had graced the ceilings of Rosewind. A Queen Anne-style mansion also in Superior, Rosewind was built at virtually the same time as Fairlawn. It is also known as the "Captain Barker House"—and therein lies a story.

Captain Charles S. Barker and Martin Pattison were contemporaries, but by no means were they friends. By all accounts, in fact, they had very little use for one another. Barker was in charge of maintaining and improving navigation in Superior's harbor, and as the story goes, he purposely directed his barges to dump their dredge spoils—some 22 million cubic yards' worth—near shore directly in front of Fairlawn. In other words, he intended to ruin Pattison's view of Lake Superior and thereby get his goat.

Over time, this accretion became known as Barker's Island, now the site of a marina and hotel complex as well as the *S.S. Meteor* Museum. Many visitors to Fairlawn, seeing the view as it appears today, have wondered at Martin Pattison's choice of real estate, but when the mansion was built the prospect it afforded of Lake Superior was commanding—

Above: The four quadrants of ceiling surrounding the center oval were painted on canvas and attached to the dining room ceiling.

Opposite: The sitting room ceiling.

and completely unimpeded. So perhaps there is some poetic justice—or at least poetic irony—in the fact that Captain Barker's chandeliers now hang in Martin Pattison's home.

For the remainder of the interior lighting, Gail Winkler had to look no further than Charles Neri Antiques, dealers in antique fixtures who, like her, are headquartered in Philadelphia. With the fixtures as they appear in the Barry and Greenfield photographs as her guide, Winkler scoured Neri's inventory for pieces that, while not exact duplicates of the originals, closely matched their scale, splendor, and configuration. She would then send photographs of these pieces to Rachael Martin for comment and approval. Winkler and Martin served as the interior design team, making the decisions on lighting and fabric—subject to the constraints of their budget, of course.

Winkler and Martin served as the interior design team, making the decisions on lighting and fabrics—subject to the constraints of their budget, of course.

When the Neri order was completed, topped by the spectacular "bowl" chandelier Winkler selected for the dining room—spectacular to the tune of $6,500, wholesale—the firm dispatched its own truck from Philadelphia to make the delivery. The substantial size of the order was one reason for this personalized service. Another was the fact that Christopher Neri, son of Charles, is an ardent birder with a special passion for raptors, and the Duluth-Superior area is renowned in the ornithological community for its opportunities to observe species such as the gyrfalcon, northern hawk owl, and boreal owl that are rarely

sighted elsewhere in the United States. As someone who possessed a keen interest in birds and all natural history, Martin Pattison would undoubtedly be pleased by this connection.

Another of Winkler's mainstays, Museum Quality Restorations of Salem, New Jersey, repaired the damaged lantern at the rear of the main hallway. This firm also supplied all of the ornamental poles for the curtains and portieres, reproduced as accurately as possible based on what could be gleaned from the old photographs. Indeed, enlargements of these photographs made by Martin and then-DCHS collections manager Joe Korman were of invaluable assistance to all of the parties involved in crafting Fairlawn's textiles.

For a variety of reasons, including cost and the absence of any samples of the original materials, woven-to-order reproductions of the Pattison-era draperies were not an option. But while Winkler acknowledges that the fabrics were purchased "off the rack," in this case off the rack means from purveyors of the finest damasks. In fact, the majority of the fabrics Winkler ultimately selected—guided, again, by the photographic evidence as well as by Furhoff's documentation of the original color schemes—were woven in Italy.

Drapery construction was entrusted to an artisan somewhat closer to the "action," Colleen Shaul, the proprietor of the Window Mill in, yes, Superior. The detail provided by the enlarged photographs enabled her to be uncannily accurate, down to matching the number of curtain rings and pleats in the originals. When it came time to sew on the elaborate trims, which had been custom-made to Winkler's specifications by Scalamandre Silks, Inc., of Long Island City, New York, Rachael Martin issued a call for experienced needleworkers to tackle the job. A number of skilled individuals from the Superior area (all women, as it happened) responded, and for a period of several weeks, working under Shaul's direction in an improvised studio on Fairlawn's third floor, their fingers flew as they stitched the rich cording, ball, and ball-and-tassel trims to the curtains—exactly as it had been done a century earlier.

Another Superior craftsperson, David Ross of David's Upholstery, was hired to re-

Pages 96-97: Two views of the stair landing.

Opposite: Pattison family heirlooms both, the statue of Pandora graces the parlor and the painted screen depicting the four seasons sits in the music room entrance.

cover banquettes (benches built into the walls) in the parlor and library, the former in bullion-fringed damask, the latter in a mohair plush. Ross also helped to re-create a second parlor banquette that had been removed, presumably during the children's home era.

Most of this work was going on during the late autumn of 1998 and the winter of 1998-99. In fact, by far the larger portion of the restoration's decorative arts component transpired *after* the mansion's "official" reopening celebration on October 24, 1998. While it would have been more timely for this event to be postponed until the finishing touches had been put on, the date had been set many months earlier, when it was anticipated that the project would be largely wrapped up. (Unforeseen delays are pretty much a fact of life in projects of this magnitude and complexity, especially when such a far-flung network of suppliers is involved.) Combined with the difficulty of simply finding *any* date that was suitable for most of the local dignitaries and "major players," notably the peripatetic Tom Jeffris, it was decided to go ahead with the ceremony as planned. The decision was also influenced by the fact that 1998 was the year of Wisconsin's sesquicentennial, and as noted previously, the Fairlawn restoration was the City of Superior's official sesquicentennial project.

It was a gala affair—and a proud moment for DCHS, the City of Superior, and everyone who, in however large or small a way, had helped to make the restoration a reality. But there was also a somber note to the proceedings, a note struck by the absence of an individ-

Above: No detail was overlooked by design historian Gail Caskey Winkler in re-creating the style of the original carpeting and curtains.

Opposite: The sitting room looking toward the front door.

Pages 100-101: Two views of the library, showing the bay window seat with its privacy curtains. Note the photograph on Page 39 for comparison.

ual who had made as significant a contribution as anyone. On August 4, 1998, restoration architect David Evans, at the age of only 50, succumbed to a heart attack. The news of his passing came as an "absolute shock," recalls Tom Jeffris, a sentiment echoed by Gail Winkler.

"It was awful," she says, noting that he left behind a wife and two children as well as a partner, Michael Quinn, with whom he'd been friends since college. "David Evans was one of the most sensitive architects in dealing with historic structures that I've ever worked with. Unlike many architects, he was not a prima donna. He loved to work as part of a team. By going into a project from the beginning with people who had various areas of expertise, it helped us all to have a better sense of how the building went together.

"And he was so good when he was asked to 'intervene' by adding new features to historic structures. The handicapped-accessible ramp he designed for the porte-cochere entrance at Fairlawn looks like it's always been there, and that's just one of several examples I could mention."

This book is dedicated to David Evans—just as Fairlawn itself stands today as a lasting monument to his talent, vision, and passionate commitment to historic preservation.

Although rocked by the loss of one of their visionary leaders, the Fairlawn team soldiered on—especially with the fruits of their labor so evident at this point.

The Pattisons had covered Fairlawn's floors with elaborately patterned carpets, and in an attempt to duplicate these designs as closely as possible, Winkler turned to the exhaustive archives of Woodward Grosvenor, a mill in the historic weaving center of Kidderminster, England. Winkler values highly this rare repository of carpet mill designs, some of which date to the late 18th century.

"What we discovered," she says, "is that the colors in the original designs (found in the mill archives) corresponded almost perfectly to the color schemes Bob Furhoff had established for those respective rooms. This tells us that the Pattisons were following the 'high style' of the times."

Opposite: The sitting room, looking into the library.

Armed with samples of each pattern in a number of shades, Winkler traveled to Superior, where she and Rachael Martin spent two days fine-tuning the exact colors to be specified. "Because there are subtle differences in lighting depending on the source and the time of day," Winkler explains, "it's very important to see which shade works best in a particular room."

After Woodward Grosvenor had woven the carpets (also their decorative borders), they were shipped to the Gfroerer Carpet Co. of Cincinnati, Ohio—the only firm Winkler trusts for such exacting work. The carpets proper, which had come off the loom in 27-inch-wide strips, were hand-seamed in Cincinnati before Bob Gfroerer himself trucked them to Superior for installation. There, he hand-stitched the decorative borders in place to ensure that they unerringly matched the footprint of each room—a demanding task, given the number of bays, fireplaces, and other irregular contours to be accommodated. Not only was the job demanding, it was sizable, requiring two trips on Gfroerer's part.

Because Winkler's primary responsibility was, in her words, "the surround," her role in selecting appropriate furniture for the restored rooms was essentially an advisory one. It was also the case that there was no money in the budget for acquisition of furniture or other *objets d'art*, whether antiques of the correct style and vintage or historically accurate reproductions (although such acquisition had been recommended as a long-term objective in Winkler's portion of the master plan). Most of the pieces currently gracing Fairlawn's rooms—deemed suitable substitutes for the Pattisons' originals—were donated over the years to the Douglas County Historical Society's collections by residents of the Superior area. Although DCHS lost its status as caretaker of Fairlawn shortly after the reopening, its collections continue to be displayed there by virtue of an ongoing lease arrangement.

As noted previously, however, a few *objets d'art* original to Fairlawn have been repatriated thanks to the generosity of the Pattison descendants. The two most important of

Pages 106-107: Two views of the music room. In the photograph on Page 107 can be seen the interior of the turret, through the parlor.

Opposite: The spectacular chandelier in the dining room is among several Gail Winkler found at Charles Neri Antiques in Philadelphia that closely resemble Fairlawn's original light fixtures.

these are the neo-classical marble sculpture of Pandora by noted 19th century artist Chauncey Bradley Ives, who was American-born but spent most of his working life in Italy, and the unusual (albeit unattributed) hand-painted velvet screen depicting the four seasons. Both of these works were in need of cleaning and basic conservation; in addition, the sculpture was missing parts of a thumb and three fingers. Upon Winkler's recommendation, the two pieces were entrusted to the Upper Midwest Conservation Association in Minneapolis, where art conservator Barbara Johnson made the necessary repairs to Pandora and gave them both a new lease on life.

They were returned to the same spots in Fairlawn that the Barry photos indicate they originally occupied, the statue in the parlor, the screen in the music room. Given Pandora's role in Greek mythology as the agent responsible for loosing all human ills into

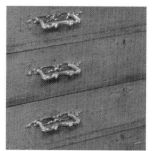

The dining room and its details.

the world by opening the forbidden box, it's faintly ironic that the parlor now serves as a popular site for brides and grooms to exchange their wedding vows.

Finding that she had a little money left in her budget, Winkler insisted that it go toward preserving another work of art: The ceiling painting in Martin Pattison's office. Although the painting was in remarkably good condition, all things considered, the ceiling plaster had sustained some significant damage and was in real danger of being lost altogether. Robert Furhoff had already surveyed the ceiling and made recommendations for its conservation, and he and Winkler were in complete agreement about who they wanted for the

The porte-cochere entrance as seen from the main hall.

job: Ron Koenig of Lansing, Michigan. Koenig, who studied under Winkler at the University of Pennsylvania, where she is an adjunct professor in the historic preservation program in the Graduate School of Fine Arts, is regarded as one of the country's top architectural art conservators. And when Winkler, whom Koenig refers to as "a dear friend and mentor," approached him about Fairlawn, he accepted without hesitation.

Accompanied by assistant conservator Esther Hernandez, Koenig made two trips to Fairlawn in the summer of 1999. (As an aside, their first visit coincided with a near-record heat wave that made things on the scaffold more than a little toasty. In Koenig's words, "It had to be 120 degrees up there.") There were four main problems that had to be addressed: The generally "grimy" condition of the painted surface; the two-by-four framing nailed into the plaster at the base of the frieze (the non-historic "drop" ceiling had been attached to this); several areas of cracked plaster and plaster that had separated from the underlying laths; and the collapse of one corner of the ceiling due to water damage.

To clean the painted surface, Koenig used a product called a Wishab, a "dry" cleaning method that, as he puts it, "works a little like a pencil eraser." He estimates that he was able to remove 75 percent to 80 percent of the dirt with this technique. The remainder was too deeply embedded to remove given his time and budget constraints (it was essentially a labor of love on his part) and the terrifically fragile nature of the paint itself, a water-soluble distemper that, if you made the mistake of wiping it with a damp cloth, would "come right off."

The two-by-fours were removed with a special cutting tool so as not to harm the plaster underneath, and the tenpenny nails that had fastened them were pulled "very gingerly," Koenig stresses. In the areas where the plaster was sagging, Koenig drilled 1/16-in. holes and injected Rhoplex, a product that penetrates and solidifies crumbling plaster and causes it to re-adhere to the underlying drywall.

Finally, Koenig replastered the missing corner section. Then, after applying a primer coat of Rhoplex, he re-created the "lost" painting, albeit in acrylics, not water-based tempera. "The idea," he explains, "is for it to blend in aesthetically, but not to be mistaken as original. When you do this kind of painting in an historic building, you 'flag' it so that on close inspection you can tell the old work from the new." Clearly, he follows the same basic principle that guided the design of the enclosed fire-rated stairwell on the south elevation of the mansion.

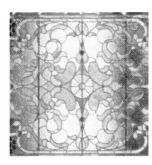

The conservation of the ceiling in Martin Pattison's office brought the restoration of Fairlawn—this chapter of it, at least—to a close. Some $1.7 million in hard cash had been invested in the project, but it would be impossible to put a price tag on the value of the time, labor, and expertise that were either donated outright or vastly exceeded the scope of contracted services. The bottom line is that a great many people, in Superior and elsewhere, believed that restoring Fairlawn was vitally important, and the financial support—the largesse of the Jeffris Foundation in particular—was merely the catalyst that set these human resources into motion.

The dream of restoring Fairlawn's splendor was achieved by dozens of talented people focusing on the small details.

Given "an opportunity to dream," as Marshall Weems so eloquently put it, the residents of Superior and Douglas County can now point with pride to an historic home that stands shoulder to shoulder not only with any in Wisconsin, but with any in the entire Midwest. The thousands of visitors who flock to Fairlawn from every corner of the globe would certainly endorse this assessment; it is a truly overwhelming experience—if not a dizzying one—to stand in the midst of such palpable grandeur and try to soak it all in. It's said that the devil is in the details, but touring Fairlawn you're hard-pressed to find even the smallest, most seemingly insignificant detail that's been overlooked—just the way Martin and Grace Pattison insisted it be done from the very beginning, when they envisioned the towering castle-like home that would be a monument to their wealth, taste, and station.

Which it was—and is. More than that, though, Fairlawn is the physical embodiment of the spirit of an age. It was a time in America when no dream was too fantastic, no ambition too lofty, no barrier insurmountable. And it was a time in Superior when its citizens truly believed that their city was poised to take its place, front and center, on the world's stage. That Fairlawn has endured, when so many other Victorians have not, shows that an ember of the old Superior has continued to burn, the fire kept alive from one generation to the next by people who would not let it die.

Of course, there is a sense in which a project such as this is never truly "finished," but is instead perpetually ongoing. Restoring the rest of Martin Pattison's office is at the top of the "to-do" list—again, it is hoped that the proceeds from this book will help kick-start that endeavor—and beyond that are a myriad of worthy long-term goals identified in the master plan: Restorations of the second- and third-floor interiors, rebuilding the conservatory and carriage house, installing an iron fence similar to the one that originally enclosed the property ... the list goes on. For now, though, the order of the day is to sit back and simply enjoy the fruits of this vast—and vastly rewarding—labor.

Today, from the front steps of Fairlawn, much of the view would seem strange, if not utterly alien, to Martin Pattison—and he would surely curse Captain Barker, his old nemesis, under his breath. But upon opening those "massive mahogany portals" and stepping through the vestibule with the initials "MP" inlaid in the mosaic-tiled floor to stand in the breathtaking splendor of the main hall, he would undoubtedly feel right at home. ◆

Opposite: Martin Pattison, upon opening the mahogany front doors today, would feel right at home a century after building his splendid Fairlawn.

FAIRLAWN

THE VAST MAJORITY OF SOURCE MATERIAL regarding Martin Pattison, the Pattison family, and the early days of Fairlawn came from the archives of the Douglas County Historical Society. Historical accounts of the life of Martin Pattison differ with respect to certain dates and places; in these instances, every effort was made to utilize what was judged to be the best, most reliable information. However, no guarantee of accuracy is possible.

The following sources were consulted for general historical background about the Lake Superior region, the founding of the City of Superior, and its development during Martin Pattison's lifetime:

BOOKS
Ashworth, William. *The Late, Great Lakes: An Environmental History*. New York: Alfred A. Knopf, 1986.
McKee, Russell. *Great Lakes Country*. New York: Crowell, 1966.
Seno, William Joseph, ed. and comp. *Up Country: Voices from the Midwestern Wilderness*. Madison, Wis.: Round River, 1985.

ARTICLES
City of Superior. *Report of the City Statistician for 1892*. Superior, Wis, 1893.
City of Superior Department of Community Development. *Superior Intensive Survey Report*. By Paul R. Lusignan. Superior, Wis., 1983.

Information regarding the architectural and decorative details of Fairlawn, as well as the steps involved in the restoration, was assembled via telephone and personal interviews (see Acknowledgments), site visits, and further research in the archives of the Douglas County Historical Society. The single most comprehensive source for such information, however, was the Master Plan for Restoration, prepared for the DCHS under the title "Fairlawn Mansion and Museum Project" and dated October 5, 1996. This included both the Historic Structure Report developed by Quinn Evans/Architects and the Decorative Arts Report written by Gail Winkler. Hugh Bishop's article "Elegance Unveiled" in the November 1999 issue of *Lake Superior* magazine was also very helpful.

Acknowledgments

Many individuals assisted the author in the course of his research and writing, and they are due much credit. Two people who deserve particular mention are James Brew, vice president of LHB Engineers & Architects and Architect of Record for the Fairlawn restoration, and Richard Sauers, former executive director of Superior Public Museums, Inc. Both were unstintingly helpful in responding to my queries—and I have no doubt that they are both extremely relieved, now that I'm no longer pestering them, to be getting some real work done for a change. Charlie Cieslak, who as the Fairlawn project coordinator for the City of Superior has probably "lived" with the mansion longer than anyone, was another invaluable source of information.

Almost all of the key players in the restoration process, whether on the administrative/financial side or the design/build side, willingly carved time out of their busy schedules so I could interview them. My thanks to Marshall Weems, former director of planning for the City of Superior; Margaret Ciccone, mayor of Superior from 1995 to mid-2000; "paint detective" Robert Furhoff; Gail Caskey Winkler, design historian specializing in 19th century interiors; Dave Strickland of Affiliated Artists; and art conservator Ron Koenig.

Nancy Minahan, Bill Rehnstrand, Leigh Cherry, Jeanne Frodesen, and Jim Pellman were among the members of the Douglas County Historical Society who, in addition to providing mountains of photos, documents, and other material relevant to Fairlawn and the Pattison family, offered valuable insights into local history in general and the restoration specifically. They also extended hospitality to me during the several days I spent "holed up" in the society's archives.

Of course, were it not for the vision and generosity of Tom Jeffris of the Jeffris Family Foundation, this book would never have seen the light of day. Wisconsin's historic restoration community is truly fortunate to have such an enthusiastic benefactor. I am grateful as well to Anita Matcha of Trails Media Group, Inc. for inviting me to author this volume. I can only hope that I've justified her confidence in my abilities.

Finally, an especially heartfelt thank you to my editor, Judith Ettenhofer, for her exceptional wisdom, patience, and humor. Every writer should be so fortunate.

Tom Davis